SOLUTIONS TO EXERCISES IN

Intermediate Statistical Methods

SOLUTIONS TO EXERCISES IN

Intermediate Statistical Methods

G. BARRIE WETHERILL
Professor of Statistics,
University of Kent at Canterbury

LONDON NEW YORK
CHAPMAN AND HALL

First published 1981 by
Chapman and Hall Ltd
11 New Fetter Lane, London EC4P 4EE

Published in the USA by
Chapman and Hall
in association with Methuen, Inc.
733 Third Avenue, New York NY 10017

Printed in Great Britain by
Whitstable Litho Ltd, Whitstable, Kent

ISBN 0 412 23520 X

British Library Cataloguing in Publication Data

Wetherill, G. Barrie
Solution to exercises in Intermediate statistical methods
1. Mathematical statistics — Examinations, questions, etc.
I. Title II. Intermediate statistical methods
519.5'07 QA276.2 80-42278

ISBN 0-412-23520-X

Contents

INTRODUCTION

This booklet contains hints to the solutions and answers where necessary, of the exercises contained in 'Intermediate Statistical Methods' by G. Barrie Wetherill. The following principles have been adopted in dealing with the answers.

(1) In some cases the answer is the drawing of a graph, and this has been omitted.

(2) In many numerical exercises a considerable amount of 'data snooping', plotting of residuals, etc. should follow the main analysis. The inclusion of this material would make the answer booklet far too long.

(3) In some cases there is a readily available reference from which the answer can be obtained, in which case reference has been made to this.

It is not necessary to work through every exercise , but it should be recognised that the exercises are an integral part of the main text, and a comprehensive grasp of the subject cannot be obtained without attempting a substantial proportion of them. It is hoped that this booklet will be of assistance in pointing the way, and providing a check on the more vital calculations.

The importance of numerical exercises should be stressed, and it is here that Appendix *B* is of importance. There is abundant material available there in many different fields of application. Currently we are in the process of mounting a form of Appendix *B* on a computer, together with accessing programs.

Many people have assisted me with this booklet, but particularly Mr. P. Duncombe, Mr. T.M.M. Farley, Mr. P. Gilbert. Messrs.K.Daffin, K. Darby and A.T. Taylor have also assisted.

CHAPTER ONE

Some Properties of Basic Statistical Procedures

EXERCISES 1.2

1. The difference of the two means $(\mu_{1,A} - \mu_{1,B})$ is distributed normally. Therefore a 95% confidence interval is given by

$$(\bar{x}_{1,A} - \bar{x}_{1,B}) \pm 2.145 \{\text{standard error of } (\bar{x}_{1,A} - \bar{x}_{1,B})$$

where 2.145 is the 95% point of the t-distribution on 14 d.f. We have already calculated (in Ex.1.8) that

$$(\bar{x}_{1,A} - \bar{x}_{1,B}) = 0.7713$$

Standard error = 0.4682 .

The required confidence interval is thus

$$0.7713 \pm 2.145 \times 0.4682 = -0.233, 1.776 .$$

2. We proceed by observing that

$$(\mu_{1,A} - \mu_{2,B} - \mu_{1,B} + \mu_{2,B}) = (\mu_{1,A} - \mu_{1,B}) - (\mu_{2,A} - \mu_{2,B}) .$$

The argument in (ii) on page 7 is extended by the use of the assumption

$$\sigma^2_{1A} = \sigma^2_{1B} = \sigma^2_{2A} = \sigma^2_{2B} = \sigma^2.$$

This exercise tests the hypothesis that the treatment effect is the same in each laboratory, i.e. that there is no interaction effect between the treatment and the laboratory in which it is given. In such a case the distribution of $(\mu_{1,A} - \mu_{1,B})$ should be the same as the distribution of $(\mu_{2,A} - \mu_{2,B})$.

EXERCISES 1.4

1., 2., 3. These are practical exercises which involve the drawing of the graphs stated. The ideas behind these exercises are to show the tendency of the t and χ^2 distributions to normality, and to gain some experience which will be helpful in interpreting normal plots.

EXERCISES 1.5

1. From the first part of the question:

$$s^4 = \frac{1}{n^2} \sum_i (X_i-\mu)^4 + \frac{2[(n-1)^2+2]}{n^2(n-1)^2} \sum_{i<j}\sum (X_i-\mu)^2(X_j-\mu)^2$$
$$+ \text{ terms involving } (X_i-\mu) .$$

Taking expectations, all terms involving $(X_i-\mu)$ are zero since $E(X_i) = \mu$

$$E(s^4) = \frac{1}{n^2}\sum_i E(X_i-\mu)^4 + \frac{2[(n-1)^2+2]}{n^2(n-1)^2} \sum_{i<j}\sum E(X_i-\mu)^2 E(X_j-\mu)^2$$

since $(X_i-\mu)$ and $(X_j-\mu)$ are independent.

But $E(X_i-\mu)^4 = (\sigma_2+3)\sigma^4$

and $E(X_i-\mu)^2E(X_j-\mu)^2 = \sigma^4$

Hence:

$$E(s^4) = \frac{n(\gamma_2+3)\sigma^4}{n^2} + \frac{2[(n-1)^2+2]}{n^2(n-1)^2} \cdot \frac{n(n-1)}{2}\sigma^4$$

$$E(s^4) = \frac{(\gamma_2+3)\sigma^4}{n} + \frac{(n^2-2n+3)}{n(n-1)}\sigma^4$$

Hence:

$$V(s^2) = E(s^4) - \sigma^4 = \left\{\frac{(n-1)(\gamma_2+3) + (n^2-2n+3) - n(n-1)}{n(n-1)}\right\}\sigma^4$$

$$= \frac{\{\gamma_2(n-1) + 2n\}}{n(n-1)}\sigma^4 .$$

EXERCISES 1.10

1. The tests which should be included are similar to examples a[n]d previous exercises given in the chapter:

(a) See Ex.1.4.

(b) See Ex.1.8.

(c) See Exercise 1.2.1.

(d) This could be tested by considering $(\bar{x}_{1A}+\bar{x}_{1B}) - (\bar{x}_{2A}+\bar{x}_{2B})$.

(e) See Ex.1.9.

C H A P T E R   T W O

Regression and the Linear Model

EXERCISES 2.1

1. Many examples are possible. Using those from the text, and from the list in §8.2:

(i) Linear parameters, linear explanatory variable

$$Y_i = \alpha + \beta t_i + e_i.$$

(ii) Linear parameters, non-linear variable

$$E(Y_i) = \alpha + \beta e^{-t_i}$$

or

$$E(Y_i) = \alpha + \beta x_i + \gamma x_i^2.$$

(iii) Non-linear parameters, linear variable

$$E(Y_i) = \alpha + x \sin \Theta .$$

(iv) Non-linear parameters, non-linear variable

$$E(Y_i) = \alpha + \beta e^{-\gamma t_i}.$$

2. The model is $E(Y_1) = \Theta_A$, $E(Y_2) = \Theta_B$, $E(Y_3) = \Theta_A + \Theta_B$, $V(Y_i) = \sigma^2$, $i = 1,2,3$ and Y's uncorrelated. Thus

$$E(\tfrac{1}{2}Y_1 + \tfrac{1}{2}(Y_3 - Y_2)) = \tfrac{1}{2}E(Y_1) + \tfrac{1}{2}(E(Y_3) - E(Y_2)) = \Theta_A$$

and

$$V(\tfrac{1}{2}Y_1 + \tfrac{1}{2}(Y_3 - Y_2)) = \tfrac{1}{4}\{V(Y_1) + V(Y_2) + V(Y_3)\} = \tfrac{3}{4}\sigma^2$$

Let $a_1Y_1 + a_2Y_2 + a_3Y_3$ be a linear unbiased estimator of Θ_A; then a_1, a_2, a_3 must satisfy

$$E(a_1Y_1 + a_2Y_2 + a_3Y_3) = \Theta_A$$

i.e. $(a_1 + a_3)\Theta_A + (a_2 + a_3)\Theta_B = \Theta_A$.

Hence $a_2 = -a_3$ and $a_3 = 1 - a_1$.

Therefore any linear unbiased estimator of Θ_A is of the form

$$cY_1 + (1-c)(Y_3 - Y_2) .$$

Its variance is given by

2. cont'd.

$$\{c^2 + 2(1-c)^2\}\sigma^2 = (3c^2-4c+2)\sigma^2 \ .$$

This is minimized when $c = \frac{2}{3}$, giving $\frac{1}{3}Y + \frac{1}{3}(Y_3 - Y_2)$ as the *MVLUE* of Θ_A with variance $\frac{2}{3}\sigma^2$.

3. Given $E(Y_1) = \Theta_A \quad E(Y_2) = \Theta_B \quad E(Y_3) = \Theta_A + \Theta_B$

$$E\{a_1Y_1 + a_2Y_2 + a_3Y_3\} = a_1\Theta_A + a_2\Theta_B + a_3(\Theta_A+\Theta_B)$$
$$= (a_1+a_3)\Theta_A + (a_2+a_3)\Theta_B .$$

$\therefore$ Condition necessary is

$$a_1 + a_3 = \alpha$$
$$a_2 + a_3 = \beta .$$

$\therefore$ A linear unbiased estimate of $(\alpha\Theta_A+\beta\Theta_B)$ is

$$Z = (\alpha-a_3)Y_1 + (\beta-a_3)Y_2 + a_3Y_3$$
$$V(Z) = \{(\alpha-a_3)^2 + (\beta-a_3)^2 + a_3^2\}\sigma^2$$
$$\frac{dV}{da_3} = \sigma^2\{-2(\alpha-a_3) - 2(\beta-a_3) + 2a_3\} .$$

This is a minimum if

$$6a_3 = 2\alpha + 2\beta$$
$$a_3 = \tfrac{1}{3}(\alpha+\beta) \quad \therefore \begin{cases} a_1 = \tfrac{1}{3}(2\alpha-\beta) \\ a_2 = \tfrac{1}{3}(2\beta-\alpha) \end{cases} .$$

Now *MVLUE* of Θ_A is

$$\tfrac{2}{3}Y_1 + \tfrac{1}{3}(Y_3-Y_2)$$

and *MVLUE* of Θ_B is

$$\tfrac{2}{3}Y_2 + \tfrac{1}{3}(Y_3-Y_1) .$$

From this the result follows.

EXERCISES 2.2

1. This result follows from the algebra above (2.11), which shows that

$$S = \Sigma\{y_i - \bar{y} - \beta(x_i - \bar{x})\}$$
$$= CS(y,y) - 2\beta CS(x,y) + \beta^2 CS(x,x) .$$

2. Calculations required for fitting the regression line of y on x by least squares.

	y	xy	x
Total	621	-	763
Mean	56.454	-	69.364
USS or USP	36639	44891	57133
Correction	35058.273	43074.818	52924.454
CSS or CSP	1580.727	1816.182	4208.545

2 cont'd.

$$\hat{\beta} = CS(x,y)/CS(x,x) = 0.4315$$

$$\hat{\alpha} = \bar{y} - \hat{\beta}\bar{x} = 26.520.$$

The fitted regression line is thus

$$y = 26.520 + 0.4315\, x$$

$$S_{min} = 1580.727 - \frac{(1816.182)^2}{4208.545}$$

$$S_{min} = 796.960.$$

EXERCISES 2.3

1. This is fully covered in the reference given (Wetherill, 1972, p.230-1).

2. Now

$$\hat{\beta} = \frac{1}{CS(x,x)} \{\Sigma(x_i - \bar{x})y_i + \Sigma(x_i - \bar{x})\bar{y}\} = \frac{1}{CS(x,x)} \Sigma(x_i - \bar{x})y_i$$

since $\Sigma(x_i - \bar{x})\bar{y} = 0$.

$$\therefore \quad C(y_j, \hat{\beta}) = \frac{1}{CS(x,x)} \sum_{i=1}^{n} (x_i - \bar{x})C(y_j, y_i)$$

$$= \frac{(x_j - \bar{x})\sigma^2}{CS(x,x)} .$$

By summing over i we get the result.

3. Let us use the model

$$E(Y_i) = \alpha + \beta(x_i - \bar{x})$$

$$V(Y_i) = \sigma^2$$

$$R_i = Y_i - \bar{Y} - \hat{\beta}(X_i - \bar{X})$$

$$E(R_i) = \alpha + \beta(X_i - \bar{X}) - \alpha - \beta(X_i - \bar{X}) = 0 .$$

$$V(R_i) = V(Y_i) + V(\bar{Y}) + (X_i - \bar{X})^2 V(\hat{\beta}) - 2C(Y_i, \bar{Y}) - 2(X_i - \bar{X})C(Y_i, \hat{\beta})$$

$$= \sigma^2 + \frac{\sigma^2}{n} + \frac{(X_i - \bar{X})^2\sigma^2}{CS(x,x)} - \frac{2\sigma^2}{n} - \frac{2(X_i - \bar{X})^2\sigma^2}{n}$$

$$= \sigma^2\left(1 - \frac{1}{n} - \frac{(x_i - \bar{x})^2}{CS(x,x)}\right)$$

$$C(R_i, R_j) = C(Y_i - \bar{Y} - \hat{\beta}(X_i - \bar{X}),\ Y_j - \bar{Y} - \hat{\beta}(X_j - \bar{X}))$$

$$= C(Y_i, Y_j) - C(Y_i, \bar{Y}) - (X_j - \bar{X})C(Y_i, \hat{\beta})$$

$$- C(\bar{Y}, Y_j) + V(\bar{Y}) + (X_j - \bar{X})C(\bar{Y}, \hat{\beta})$$

$$- (X_i - \bar{X})C(Y_j, \hat{\beta}) + (X_i - \bar{X})C(\hat{\beta}, \bar{Y}) + (X_j - \bar{X})(X_i - \bar{X})V(\hat{\beta})$$

$$= -\frac{\sigma^2}{n} - \frac{(X_j - \bar{X})(X_i - \bar{X})\sigma^2}{CS(x,x)} - \frac{\sigma^2}{n} + \frac{\sigma^2}{n}$$

3 cont'd.

$$= -\frac{\sigma^2}{n} - \frac{(X_i - \bar{X})(X_j - \bar{X})}{CS(x,x)}$$

4. The fitted regression line is $y = \hat{\alpha} + \hat{\beta}x$ and the intercept of the regression line on the Y axis is given by

$$y = \hat{\alpha} = \bar{y} - \hat{\beta}\bar{x} .$$

The variance of the intercept is

$$V(\bar{Y} - \hat{\beta}\bar{x}) = \frac{\sigma^2}{n} + \bar{x}^2 V(\hat{\beta}) = \sigma^2\left(\frac{1}{n} + \frac{\bar{x}^2}{CS(x,x)}\right) .$$

For Example 2.1, using the results in Table 2.1, we find that the intercept on the Y axis is 1.4125. Its variance is given by $0.28607\sigma^2$. Since σ^2 is not known we must estimate it by $S_{min}/(n-2)$ and use the t-distribution on 9 d.f. to construct a confidence interval. Thus the 95% C.I. for the intercept on the Y axis is given by

$$1.4125 \pm t_9(95\%) \times \sqrt{0.28607 \times \frac{0.002655}{9}}$$
$$= 1.4125 \pm 0.0208$$
$$= (1.3917, 1.4333)$$

EXERCISES 2.4

1. A normal plot would be sufficient.

2. The answers are in Table 5.2.

3. From (2.25) the variance is given by

$$\sigma^2\left\{\frac{1}{n} + \frac{(x' - \bar{x})^2}{CS(x,x)}\right\} \text{ at point } x_i = x' .$$

Using the estimate of σ^2, $\sigma^2 = 0.000295$, we have

$$\text{Variance} = 0.000295\left\{\frac{1}{11} + \frac{(x' - 35.8182)^2}{6573.6364}\right\}$$

t	$\hat{Y}_i$	$V(\hat{Y}_i)$	$Std. Dev(\hat{Y}_i)$	95% limits
5	1.4007	0.000069	0.0083	(1.3844,1.4170)
20	1.3654	0.000038	0.0062	(1.3532,1.3776)
30	1.3418	0.000028	0.0053	(1.3314,1.3522)
50	1.2947	0.000036	0.0060	(1.2829,1.3065)
70	1.2475	0.000079	0.0089	(1.2301,1.2649)

4. The residuals should be checked for outliers. Plots of residuals should be made as indicated in Fig.2.3, and a normal plot would be satisfactory for a check of normality.

5.

	log y(breaking load)	yx	log x(diameter)
Total	-243		-100
Mean	- 1.31351		- 0.54054
USS(USP)	1943.00000	1219	1018.00000
Correction	319.18378	131.35135	54.05405
CSS(CSP)	1623.8162	1087.6487	963.9460

$$\hat{\beta} = 1087.6487/963.9460 = 1.1283$$

$$\hat{\alpha} = -1.31351 - (-0.54054 \times 1.1283) = -0.7036$$

ANOVA

Source	CSS	d.f.	Mean Square	E(M.S.)
Due to regression	1227.194	1	1227.194	$\sigma^2+\beta^2 CS(x,x)$
Residual S.S.	396.622	183	2.167	
Total S.S.	1623.8162	184		

(ii) To see whether $\hat{\beta}$ is significantly different from 2, we use the fact that

$$\hat{\beta} \sim N(\beta, \sigma^2/CS(x,x))$$

which implies

$$\frac{\hat{\beta} - \beta}{\sigma\sqrt{CS(x,x)}} \sim t_{183}$$

If β =2 this test statistic has a value of -18.385, which is clearly highly significant.

EXERCISES 2.5

1. See notes on Exc.2.2.2 which give the regression line for y on x as

$$y = 26.520 + 0.4315x$$

using that data but regressing x on y we have

$$\hat{\beta}_{x|y} = CS(x,y)/CS(x,x) = 1.1490$$

$$\hat{\alpha}_{x|y} = \bar{x} - \hat{\beta}_{x|y}\,\bar{y} = 4.498$$

The regression line of x on y is thus

$$x = 4.498 + 1.149y$$

EXERCISES 2.6

1. We have, from (2.34)

$$R_i = y_i - \hat{\alpha} - \hat{\beta}_1(w_i - \bar{w}) - \hat{\beta}_2(x_i - \bar{x})$$

and from Ex.2.4 we have

$$\hat{\alpha} = 2.1484 \qquad \hat{\beta}_1 = 1.2473 \qquad \hat{\beta}_2 = 0.8865 \qquad \hat{\sigma}^2 = 0.00171$$

$$\bar{w} = 1.6391 \qquad \bar{x} = 1.6073 \ .$$

Using these results:

y_i	R_i
2.318	0.0567
2.100	0.0564
2.225	-0.0223
2.140	-0.0210
2.107	-0.0202
2.049	-0.0468
2.228	0.0033
2.029	0.0084
2.140	-0.0146

An indication of outliers is better provided by the calculation of standardised residuals as in Exc.2.4.2, but we note that an assumption of equal variance approximately equal to $\hat{\sigma}^2$ would give 1.37 as the value of the largest (approximate) standardised residual. It is unlikely on data such as this that differences from this assumption would produce true standardised residuals sufficiently large to give cause for concern.

The residuals can be checked for normality by doing a probability plot and for homogeneity of variance by plotting them against $\hat{y}_i$ as described in 2.4.

2. The key trick here is to notice that

$$CS(x,y) = \sum_{i=1}^{n} (x_i - \bar{x})y_i .$$

It reduces the algebra considerably. The results are stated in the answer to Exercise 5.2.3.

C H A P T E R   T H R E E

Statistical Models and Statistical Inference

EXERCISES 3.2

1. $V(s) = E(s^2) - E^2(s)$

$\therefore V(s) = \sigma^2 - E^2(s)$

$\therefore E^2(s) = \sigma^2 - V(s)$.

Since $V(s)$ is positive, $E^2(s) < \sigma^2$

$\therefore E(s) < \sigma$.

2. There are many circumstances in which the relative efficiency of two estimators is not the only consideration and sometimes not the most important consideration. Two examples are provided in the text; the use of the sample median if there is reason to suspect the occurrence of outliers, and the use of the two-group method to ease calculation. Only if all other considerations were equal could one regard relative efficiency as a true indicator of the difference between two estimators.

EXERCISES 3.3

1. $\ell(\theta) = (1-\theta)^0\,\theta\,(1-\theta)^4\theta.\ \ (1-\theta)^3\theta.\ (1-\theta)^5\theta.\ \ (1-\theta)^7\theta.$

$\ell(\theta) = (1-\theta)^{19}\ \theta^5$

$L(\theta) = 19\log(1-\theta) + 5\log\theta$

2. $\ell(\theta) = \binom{20}{0}\theta^0(1-\theta)^{20}$ [c.f. (3.6)]

$\ell(\theta) = (1-\theta)^{20}$

$L(\theta) = 20\log(1-\theta)$

3. $\ell(\lambda) = \lambda e^{-\lambda t_1}.\lambda e^{-\lambda t_2}.\lambda e^{-\lambda t_3} \ldots \lambda e^{-\lambda t_n}$

$$\ell(\lambda) = \lambda^n e^{-\lambda \sum_i^n t_i}$$

$$L(\lambda) = n \log \lambda - \lambda \sum_1^n t_i .$$

4. $\ell(\alpha) = \prod_{i=1}^{n} \alpha(\alpha x_i)^4 e^{-\alpha x_i}/24$

$$L(\alpha) = 5n \log \alpha + 4 \sum_{i=1}^{n} \log x_i - \alpha \sum_{i=1}^{n} x_i + C.$$

5. See the reference given (Cox and Hinkley, 1974, p.12).

EXERCISES 3.4

1.(a) From Ex.3.6

$$\ell(\theta) = k\theta^{18}(1-\theta)^{42}$$

$$\therefore L(\theta) = C + 18 \log \theta + 42 \log (1-\theta)$$

$$\frac{dL}{d\theta} = \frac{18}{\theta} - \frac{42}{(1-\theta)} .$$

For the likelihood to be a maximum we solve for $\frac{dL}{d\theta} = 0$ which gives $\underline{\theta = 0.3}$.

(b) From Exc.3.3.3

$$L(\lambda) = n \log \lambda - \lambda \sum_1^n t_i$$

$$\frac{dL}{d\lambda} = \frac{n}{\lambda} - \sum_1^n t_i = \frac{n}{\lambda} - n\bar{t}$$

when $\frac{dL}{d\lambda} = 0$, $\hat{\lambda} = \frac{1}{\bar{t}}$.

(c) From Exc.3.3.4

$$L(\alpha) = 5n \log \alpha + 4 \sum_1^n \log x_i - \alpha \sum_1^n x_i + C$$

$$\frac{dL}{d\alpha} = \frac{5n}{\alpha} - \sum_1^n x_i = \frac{5n}{\alpha} - n\bar{x}$$

when $\frac{dL}{d\alpha} = 0$, $\hat{\alpha} = \frac{5}{\bar{x}}$

2. If the p.d.f. is $e^{-x/\theta}/\theta$

$$\ell(\theta) = e^{-\sum_1^n x_i/\theta}/\theta^n$$

$$L(\theta) = -\sum_1^n x_i/\theta - n \log \theta$$

$$\frac{dL}{d\theta} = \frac{n\bar{x}}{\theta^2} - \frac{n}{\theta}$$

when $\frac{dL}{d\theta} = 0$, $\underline{\hat{\theta} = \bar{x}}$

2. cont'd.

We note that this is the reciprocal of the corresponding estimator in Exc.3.4.1(b).

3. The "stopping rule" makes no difference to the maximum likelihood estimate of Θ, since the difference in the probability function from an ordinary binomial situation is in the constant. We can therefore obtain the estimate by using from Ex.3.10

$$\hat{\Theta} = r/n \ .$$

This gives a value for $\hat{\Theta}$ of $^3/_{20}$ or 0.15.

EXERCISES 3.5

1. For convenience and simplicity we will put $\sigma^2 = \phi$. Then from (3.10) we have

$$L(\mu,\phi) = C - \frac{n}{2}\log\phi - \frac{1}{2\phi}\Sigma(x_i - \bar{x})^2 - \frac{n}{2\phi}(\bar{x}-\mu)^2.$$

Thus

$$\frac{\partial L}{\partial\phi} = -\frac{n}{2\phi} + \frac{1}{2\phi^2}\Sigma(x_i - \bar{x})^2 + \frac{n}{2\phi^2}(\bar{x}-\mu)^2$$

and

$$\frac{\partial^2 L}{\partial\phi^2} = \frac{n}{2\phi^2} - \frac{1}{\phi^3}\Sigma(x_i - \bar{x})^2 - \frac{n}{\phi^3}(\bar{x}-\mu)^2$$

$$E\left(\frac{\partial^2 L}{\partial\phi^2}\right) = \frac{n}{2\phi^2} - \frac{(n-1)}{\phi^2} - \frac{1}{\phi^2}$$

since $E(\Sigma(x_i - \bar{x})^2) = (n-1)\phi$ and $E(\bar{x}-\mu)^2 = V(\bar{x}) = \frac{\phi}{n}$

$$I = -E\left(\frac{\partial^2 L}{\partial\phi^2}\right) = \frac{n}{2\phi^2} \ .$$

Thus Minimum Variance of $\hat{\phi}(\hat{\sigma}^2) = \frac{1}{I} = \frac{2\phi^2}{n} = \frac{2\sigma^4}{n}$.

Also

$$\frac{\partial L}{\partial\mu} = \frac{n}{\phi}(\bar{x}-\mu) \qquad \frac{\partial^2 L}{\partial\mu^2} = -\frac{n}{\phi} \ .$$

Hence $I = \frac{n}{\phi}$

and the minimum variance of $\hat{\mu} = \frac{\phi}{n} = \frac{\sigma^2}{n}$.

2. For the exponential distribution

$$E(X) = \int_0^\infty X\frac{1}{\Theta}e^{-X/\Theta}dX = \Theta$$

$$E(X^2) = \int_0^\infty X^2\frac{1}{\Theta}e^{-X/\Theta}dX = -\int^\infty X^2\, d(e^{-X/\Theta})$$

$$E(X^2) = 2\int_0^\infty e^{-X/\Theta}X\,dX = 2\Theta^2.$$

$$\therefore \quad V(X) = E(X^2) - E^2(X) = \Theta^2$$

$$\therefore \quad V(\bar{X}) = \frac{1}{n}V(X) = \frac{\Theta^2}{n} \ ,$$

which is exactly equal to the minimum variance.

3. Given observations $r_1, r_2, r_3, \ldots, r_n$ on a Poisson distribution.

$$\ell(\mu) = e^{-n\mu} \mu^{\sum_1^n r_i} \quad r_i!$$

$$L(\mu) = - n \mu + \Sigma r_i (\log \mu) - C$$

$$\frac{dL}{d\mu} = - n + \frac{\Sigma r_i}{\mu}$$

$$\frac{\partial^2 L}{d\mu^2} = - \frac{\Sigma r_i}{\mu^2}$$

$$I = - E\left(\frac{d^2 L}{d\mu^2}\right) \quad \frac{n}{\mu}$$

Minimum variance $= \frac{1}{I} = \frac{\mu}{n}$.

4. The maximum likelihood estimator of Θ of the binomial distribution is

$\hat{\Theta} = r/n$ (see Ex.3.10) .

The Cramér-Rao lower bound is

$\frac{\Theta(1-\Theta)}{n}$ (see Ex.3.14) .

From first principles

$$V(\tfrac{r}{n}) = \frac{1}{n^2} V(r)$$

but $V(r) = n\,\Theta(1-\Theta)$

$\therefore \quad V(\frac{r}{n}) = \frac{\Theta(1-\Theta)}{n}$, which is the lower bound.

EXERCISES 3.6

1. $\ell(\underline{x};\alpha,\beta) = \alpha^{n\beta}\, \Pi x_i^{(\beta-1)} e^{-\alpha\Sigma x_i}/[\Gamma(\beta)]^n$.

If β is known

$$\ell = \alpha^{n\beta} e^{-\alpha\Sigma x_i} \Pi\, x_i^{(\beta-1)}/[\Gamma(\beta)]^n \quad .$$

Hence Σx_i is a sufficient statistic for α .

Similarly if α is known, $\prod_{i=1}^{n} x_i$ is sufficient for β .

Finally, $(\Sigma x_i, \Pi x_i)$ is jointly sufficient for (α,β).

2. The p.d.f. is

$$f(x) = \begin{cases} \Theta^{-1} & 0 < x < \Theta \\ 0 & \text{otherwise} \end{cases}$$

so therefore

$$\ell(\Theta) = \begin{cases} \Theta^{-n} & \text{if Max } x_i < \Theta \\ 0 & \text{otherwise.} \end{cases}$$

Thus Max x_i is sufficient for Θ .

EXERCISES 3.7

1. If $k = 2$

$$\underline{\Sigma} = \begin{bmatrix} \sigma_1^2 & \rho_{12}\sigma_1\sigma_2 \\ \rho_{12}\sigma_1\sigma_2 & \sigma_2^2 \end{bmatrix}.$$

Hence $|\underline{\Sigma}| = \sigma_1^2\sigma_2^2 - \rho_{12}\sigma_1\sigma_2\rho_{12}\sigma_1\sigma_2$

$$= \sigma_1^2\sigma_2^2(1-\rho_{12}^2)$$

and inverting

$$\underline{\Sigma}^{-1} = \frac{1}{\sigma_1^2\sigma_2^2(1-\rho_{12}^2)} \begin{bmatrix} \sigma_2^2 & -\rho_{12}\sigma_1\sigma_2 \\ -\rho_{12}\sigma_1\sigma_2 & \sigma_1^2 \end{bmatrix}$$

Call $\rho_{12} = \rho$ and substitute in (3.21)

$$f(x) = \frac{1}{2\pi\sigma_1\sigma_2\sqrt{(1-\rho^2)}} \exp\left[-\frac{1}{2(1-\rho^2)}\{M\}\right]$$

where $M = [(x_1-\mu_1)\ (x_2-\mu_2)] \begin{bmatrix} \frac{1}{\sigma_1^2} & \frac{-\rho}{\sigma_1\sigma_2} \\ \frac{-\rho}{\sigma_1\sigma_2} & \frac{1}{\sigma_2^2} \end{bmatrix} \begin{bmatrix} (x_1-\mu_1) \\ (x_2-\mu_2) \end{bmatrix}$

$$M = \left(\frac{x_1-\mu_1}{\sigma_1}\right)^2 - \frac{2\rho(x_1-\mu_1)(x_2-\mu_2)}{\sigma_1\sigma_2} + \left(\frac{x_2-\mu_2}{\sigma_2}\right)^2.$$

Hence (3.21) reduces to (3.19) when $k = 2$.

2. The integration here is fairly straightforward.

CHAPTER FOUR

Properties of the Method of Maximum Likelihood

EXERCISES 4.1

1. $$\ell = \prod_1^n \{e^{-i\mu}(i\mu)^{r_i}/r_i!\}$$

$$L = \sum_1^n i\mu + \sum_1^n r_i \log(\mu) + C$$

$$\frac{dL}{d\mu} = -\Sigma i + \Sigma\frac{r_i}{\mu}$$

when $\dfrac{dL}{d\mu} = 0$, $\Sigma i = \dfrac{\Sigma r_i}{\mu}$.

Hence $\hat{\mu} = \dfrac{\Sigma r_i}{\Sigma i}$

But $\Sigma i = \dfrac{n(n+1)}{2}$.

Hence $\hat{\mu} = \dfrac{2\Sigma r_i}{n(n+1)}$.

2. Conditionally on $t < T$, the p.d.f. is

$$f(t) = \frac{e^{-t/\Theta}}{(1-e^{-T/\Theta})} .$$

Therefore

$$E(t) = \int_o^T \frac{t\, e^{-t/\Theta}}{\Theta(1-e^{-T/\Theta})}\, dt$$

$$= \frac{1}{(1-e^{-T/\Theta})}\int_o^T \frac{t}{\Theta}\, e^{-t/\Theta} dt$$

$$= -\frac{1}{(1-e^{-T/\Theta})}\int_o^T t\, d(e^{-t/\Theta})$$

$$= -\frac{1}{(1-e^{-T/\Theta})}[te^{-e/\Theta}]_o^T + \frac{1}{(1-e^{-T/\Theta})}\int_o^T e^{-t/\Theta}\, dt$$

$$= -\frac{T\, e^{-T/\Theta}}{(1-e^{-T/\Theta})} + \frac{\Theta}{(1-e^{-T/\Theta})}[1-e^{-T/\Theta}] .$$

3. The easiest way to prove the result about the distribution of $Y = \Sigma X_i$ is to use moment generating functions. In order to get the p.d.f. of $Z = Y^{-1}$, we use

$$f(z) = f(y).\frac{dy}{dz},$$

and this gives the result quoted. From here a straightforward integration to get $E(z)$, and $V(z)$, gives the result.

EXERCISES 4.2

1. We are given

$$E(Y_r) = r\Theta, \; V(Y_r) = r^2\sigma^2$$

so that the likelihood is

$$\ell(\Theta) = \prod_{r=1}^{n} \frac{1}{\sqrt{2\pi}r\sigma} \exp\{-\frac{1}{2r^2\sigma^2}(y_r - r\Theta)^2\}$$

and the log-likelihood is

$$L(\Theta) = C - \log\sigma - \Sigma\frac{(y_r - r\Theta)^2}{2r^2\sigma^2}$$

$$\frac{dL}{d\Theta} = \Sigma\frac{(y_r - r\Theta)}{r\sigma^2} \qquad \therefore \; \hat{\Theta} = \frac{1}{n}\sum_{r=1}^{n}\frac{y_r}{r}$$

$$\frac{dL}{d\sigma^2} = -\frac{n}{2\sigma^2} + \Sigma\frac{(y_r - r\Theta)^2}{2r^2\sigma^4} \qquad \therefore \; \hat{\sigma}^2 = \frac{1}{n}\sum_{r=1}^{n}\frac{(y_r - r\Theta)^2}{r^2}$$

2. We are given that Y_i are Poisson, $i = 1,2,\ldots,n$, with $E(Y_i) = \beta x_i$ so that

$$\ell(\beta) = \prod_{i=1}^{n} e^{-(\beta x_i)}\frac{(\beta x_i)^{y_i}}{y_i!}$$

and the log-likelihood is

$$L(\beta) = C - \beta\Sigma x_i + \Sigma y_i(\log\beta + \log x_i)$$

$$\frac{dL}{d\beta} = -\Sigma x_i + \frac{1}{\beta}\Sigma y_i.$$

Therefore

$$\hat{\beta} = \Sigma y_i / \Sigma x_i .$$

3. From Ex.4.5, the probability that $r = 0$ is $(1-e^{-\mu})^n$. Therefore with this probability $\hat{\mu}$ is infinite. Theorem 4.2 still holds, since the probability that this will happen tends to zero as n tends to infinity. However, the small sample distribution of $\hat{\mu}$ is quite different from the asymptotic distribution for all sample sizes.

4. Let us differentiate with respect to σ^2.

$$\frac{\partial L}{\partial\sigma^2} = -\frac{n}{\sigma^2} + \frac{1}{2\sigma^4}\Sigma\{(y_{i1}-\mu_i)^2 + (y_{i2}-\mu_i)^2\}$$

$$\frac{\partial^2 L}{\partial(\sigma^2)^2} = \frac{n}{\sigma^4} - \frac{1}{\sigma^6}\Sigma\{(y_{i1}-\mu_i)^2 + (y_{i2}-\mu_i)^2\}$$

$$E\left\{\frac{\partial^2 L}{\partial(\sigma^2)^2}\right\} = \frac{n}{\sigma^4} - \frac{1}{\sigma^6}(2n\sigma^2) = -\frac{n}{\sigma^4}$$

$$V(\sigma^2) = \frac{\sigma^4}{n}.$$

4. cont'd.
Hence asymptotically $\hat{\sigma}^2$ is normal with $E(\hat{\sigma}^2) = \sigma^2/2$ and a variance which tends to zero.

For k observations at a time, we are given

$$E(Y_{ij}) = \mu_i, \quad j = 1,2, \ldots, k, \quad i = 1,2,\ldots,n.$$

$$V(Y_{ij}) = \sigma^2$$

$$\ell(\mu_i, \sigma^2) = \prod_{i=1}^{n} \frac{1}{(2\pi)^{k/2}\,\sigma^k} \exp\{-\sum_{j=1}^{k} \frac{(y_{ij}-\mu_i)^2}{2\sigma^2}\}$$

$$L(\mu_i, \sigma^2) = C - \frac{kn}{2}\log(\sigma^2) - \frac{1}{2\sigma^2}\sum_{i=1}^{n}\sum_{j=1}^{k}(y_{ij}-\mu_i)^2$$

$$\frac{\partial L}{\partial \mu_i} = \frac{1}{\sigma^2}\sum_{j=1}^{k}(y_{ij}-\mu_i) \quad \therefore \hat{\mu}_i = \frac{1}{k}\sum_{j=1}^{k} y_{ij} = \bar{y}$$

$$\frac{\partial L}{\partial \sigma^2} = -\frac{kn}{2\sigma^2} + \frac{1}{2\sigma^4}\sum_{i=1}^{n}\sum_{j=1}^{k}(y_{ij}-\mu_i)^2$$

so that $\hat{\sigma}^2 = \frac{1}{kn}\sum_{j=1}^{k}(y_{ij}-\mu_i)^2 = \frac{1}{kn}\sum_{j=1}^{k}(y_{ij}-\bar{y})^2$.

Now $E\{\sum_{j=1}^{k}(y_{ij}-\bar{y})^2\} = (k-1)\sigma^2$

so that $E(\hat{\sigma}^2) = \frac{1}{kn}(k-1)n\sigma^2 = \frac{(k-1)}{k}\sigma^2$.

5. $\ell(\Theta) = g(t,\Theta)L(\underline{X})$ where $L(\underline{X})$ is independent of Θ

$$L(\Theta) = \log\{g(t,\Theta)\} + \log\{L(\underline{X})\}$$

$\frac{dL}{d\Theta} = \frac{1}{g(t,\Theta)} \cdot \frac{dg}{d\Theta}$ since $L(\underline{X})$ is independent of Θ .

Hence $\hat{\Theta}$ is a function of t only.

EXERCISES 4.3

1. (a) The log-likelihood becomes

$$L = 15\log\lambda - 9.798\lambda - 15\log(1-e^{-1.5\lambda}).$$

A plot of L against λ provides an estimates of $\hat{\lambda}$.

(b) $\frac{dL}{d\lambda} = \frac{15}{\lambda} - 9.798 - \frac{22.5e^{-1.5\lambda}}{(1-e^{-1.5\lambda})}$.

The gradient $\frac{dL}{d\lambda}$ can be calculated at various trial values of λ and linear interpolation used to estimate $\hat{\lambda}$.

(c) This is a question of following the text, substituting actual values where appropriate. An initial estimate $\hat{\lambda}_1$ of about 1.50 may be found suitable.

2. Following a similar argument to that used in Ex.4.5 we arrive at:

$$\ell = ke^{-0\rho}(1-e^{-\rho})^{10}e^{-\frac{3\rho}{2}}(1-e^{-\frac{\rho}{2}})^{9}\,e^{-\frac{3\rho}{4}}(1-e^{-\frac{\rho}{4}})^{5}e^{-\frac{6\rho}{8}}(1-e^{-\frac{\rho}{8}})^{6}e^{-\frac{10\rho}{16}}(1-e^{-\frac{\rho}{16}})^{1}$$

[c.f.(4.10)].

Hence

$$L = C - \frac{58}{16}\rho + 10\log(1-e^{-\rho}) + 9\log(1-e^{-\frac{\rho}{2}}) + 5\log(1-e^{-\frac{\rho}{4}}) + 6\log(1-e^{-\frac{\rho}{8}}) + \log(1-e^{-\frac{\rho}{16}})$$

$$\frac{dL}{d\rho} = -\frac{58}{16} + \frac{10e^{-\rho}}{(1-e^{-\rho})} + \frac{9e^{-\frac{\rho}{2}}}{2(1-e^{-\frac{\rho}{2}})} + \frac{5e^{-\frac{\rho}{4}}}{4(1-e^{-\frac{\rho}{4}})} + \frac{6e^{-\frac{\rho}{8}}}{8(1-e^{-\frac{\rho}{8}})} + \frac{e^{-\frac{\rho}{16}}}{16(1-e^{-\frac{\rho}{16}})}$$

$$\frac{dL}{d\rho} = -\frac{58}{16} + \frac{10}{(e^{\rho}-1)} + \frac{9}{2(e^{+\frac{\rho}{2}}-1)} + \frac{5}{4(e^{+\frac{\rho}{4}}-1)} + \frac{6}{8(e^{+\frac{\rho}{8}}-1)} + \frac{1}{16(e^{+\frac{\rho}{16}}-1)} .$$

We can use this formula to calculate $\frac{dL}{d\rho}$ for specific values of and plot $\frac{dL}{d\rho}$ against ρ to obtain an approximate estimate of $\hat{\rho}$ (when $\frac{dL}{d\rho} = 0$. We might use

$\rho = 1,\quad \frac{dL}{d\rho} = 20.135$

$\rho = 3,\quad \frac{dL}{d\rho} = 1.262$

$\rho = 5,\quad \frac{dL}{d\rho} = -1.619$.

Plotting these values, we can approximate $\hat{\rho}_1 = 3.6$ we then use the iterative method (c) described in the text to improve our estimate of $\hat{\rho}$. We need

$$\frac{d^2L}{d\rho^2} = -\frac{10e^{\rho}}{(e^{\rho}-1)^2} - \frac{9e^{\frac{\rho}{2}}}{4(e^{\frac{\rho}{2}}-1)^2} - \frac{5e^{\frac{\rho}{4}}}{16(e^{\frac{\rho}{4}}-1)^2} - \frac{6e^{\frac{\rho}{8}}}{64(e^{\frac{\rho}{8}}-1)^2} - \frac{e^{\frac{\rho}{16}}}{256(e^{\frac{\rho}{16}}-1)^2}$$

Evaluating

$$\left.\frac{dL}{d\rho}\right|_{\hat{\rho}_1 = 3.6} = -0.0354$$

$$\left.\frac{d^2L}{d\rho^2}\right|_{\hat{\rho}_1 = 3.6} = -1.7121$$

and substituting in (4.28) gives

$\hat{\rho}_2 = 3.5794$

Similarly $\hat{\rho}_3 = 3.5831$

To find the asymptotic standard error we use $\hat{\sigma}^2 = -\frac{1}{\frac{d^2L}{d\rho^2}}$

$$\left.\frac{d^2L}{d\rho^2}\right|_{\hat{\rho} = 3.5831} = -1.736 .$$

Hence $\hat{\sigma}^2 = 0.576$ and $\hat{\sigma} = 0.759$.

3. If the total number of seedlings is   and the number in each category are r_{I}, ..., r_{IV} then the likelihood of the experimental results is

$$\ell = \binom{n}{r_I\ r_{II}\ r_{III}\ r_{IV}}\left(\frac{2+\Theta}{4}\right)^{r_I}\left(\frac{1-\Theta}{4}\right)^{r_{II}}\left(\frac{1-\Theta}{4}\right)^{r_{III}}\left(\frac{\Theta}{4}\right)^{r_{IV}}$$

$$\ell = \binom{n}{r_I\ r_{II}\ r_{III}\ r_{IV}}\left(\tfrac{1}{4}\right)^{(r_I + r_{II} + r_{III} + r_{IV})}$$

$$(2+\Theta)^{r_I}(1-\Theta)^{(r_{II}+r_{III})}\Theta^{r_{IV}}$$

which is of the form

$$\ell = C_0(2+\Theta)^{C_1}(1-\Theta)^{C_2}\Theta^{C_3}$$

where C_0, C_1, C_2 and C_3 are constants.

$$L = k + C_1\log(2+\Theta) + C_2\log(1-\Theta) + C_3\log\Theta$$

$$\frac{dL}{d\Theta} = \frac{C_1}{(2+\Theta)} - \frac{C_2}{(1-\Theta)} + \frac{C_3}{\Theta}\ .$$

Equating to zero and subsrituting actual values for C_1, C_2 and C_3

$$\frac{4299}{(2+\Theta)} - \frac{4022}{(1-\Theta)} + \frac{83}{\Theta} = 0\ .$$

Hence

$$-8404\,\Theta^2 - 3828\,\Theta + 166 = 0\ .$$

Taking the positive root as our estimate of $\hat{\Theta}$

$$\hat{\Theta} = 0.040.$$

EXERCISES 4.4

1. The iteration formula required here is given in (4.34).

$$\frac{\partial L}{\partial\alpha} = -\ \Sigma(\hat{\alpha} + \hat{\beta}x_i)^{-1} + \Sigma y_i(\hat{\alpha} + \hat{\beta}x_i)^{-2} \quad \text{from (4.32)}$$

and

$$\frac{\partial L}{\partial\beta} = -\ \Sigma x_i(\hat{\alpha} + \hat{\beta}x_i)^{-1} + \Sigma y_i x_i(\hat{\alpha} + \hat{\beta}x_i)^{-2} \quad \text{from (4.33).}$$

Hence

$$\frac{d^2L}{\partial\alpha^2} = \Sigma(\hat{\alpha} + \hat{\beta}x_i)^{-2} - 2\Sigma y_i(\hat{\alpha} + \hat{\beta}x_i)^{-3}$$

and

$$\frac{d^2L}{\partial\beta^2} = \Sigma x_i(\hat{\alpha} + \hat{\beta}x_i)^{-2} - 2\Sigma y_i x_i(\hat{\alpha} + \hat{\beta}x_i)^{-3}.$$

Initial estimates for α and β may be obtained by plotting y_i against x_i and fitting a line by eye, since $y_i = \alpha + \beta x_i$. These initial estimates are used to evaluate the appropriate parts of (4.34).

2. This data is taken from Sampford, M.R. and Taylor, J. (1959) 'Censored observations in randomised block experiments'. J.R.Statist. Soc. B, Vol-21, 1, p.214-237. A full discussion of the problem is provided in the reference, but briefly, initial parameter estimates are found by plotting and then an iterative procedure is used to evaluate the two estimates:

$$\hat{\mu} = -0.055$$

$$\hat{\sigma} = 0.402\ .$$

The evidence that vitamin B_{12} has an effect on the rate of action of carbon tetrachloride is clearly not significant.

3. The answer is as follows:

$$\ell = \prod_{i=1}^{n} \frac{1}{2\pi\sqrt{(1-\rho^2)}} \exp\left[-\frac{1}{2(1-\rho^2)}\{x_i^2 - 2\rho x_i y_i + y_i^2\}\right]$$

$$L = C - \frac{n}{2}\log(1-\rho^2) - \frac{1}{2(1-\rho^2)}\Sigma\{x_i^2 - 2\rho x_i y_i + y_i^2\}$$

$$\frac{dL}{d\rho} = \frac{n\rho}{(1-\rho^2)} - \frac{\rho}{(1-\rho^2)^2}\Sigma(x_i^2 - 2\rho x_i y_i + y_i^2) + \frac{1}{(1-\rho^2)}\Sigma(x_i y_i).$$

Equation to solve is therefore (multiply by $(1-\rho^2)^2$)

$$\rho(1-\rho^2) - \rho\Sigma(x_i^2 - 2\rho x_i y_i + y_i^2) + (1-\rho^2)\ \Sigma x_i y_i) = 0$$

$$\rho(1-\rho^2) - \rho\frac{1}{n}\{\Sigma x_i^2 + \Sigma\ y_i^2\} + \frac{1}{n}\Sigma x_i y_i(2\rho^2 + 1-\rho^2) = 0$$

which is the answer.

C H A P T E R   F I V E

The Method of Least Squares

EXERCISES 5.1

1. For model (2.33)

$$\theta' = (\alpha, \beta_1, \beta_2)$$

and

$$\underline{a} = \begin{pmatrix} 1 & (w_2 - \bar{w}) & (x_2 - \bar{x}) \\ 1 & (w - \bar{w}) & (x - \bar{x}) \\ \vdots & & \\ 1 & (w_9 - \bar{w}) & (x_9 - \bar{x}) \end{pmatrix} .$$

The estimates of $\hat{\theta}$ and S_{min} are given in Chapter 2.

2. The algebra for this question is simply an extension of that in question 1 above. The details are set out in Section 5.5. If there is only one explanatory variable

$$(\underline{a}'\underline{a}) = \begin{pmatrix} n & 0 \\ 0 & CS(x,x) \end{pmatrix}$$

and the result follows.

3. Here we have α known, and

$$\ell(\beta) = \prod_{i=1}^{n} \frac{1}{\sqrt{(2\pi)}\sigma x_i^{\alpha}} \exp\left\{-\frac{1}{2\sigma^2 x_i^{2\alpha}} (y_i - \beta x_i)^2\right\}$$

$$L(\beta) = C - \alpha \Sigma \log x_i - \frac{1}{2\sigma^2} \Sigma \frac{(y_i - \beta x_i)^2}{x_i^{2\alpha}} .$$

At minimum

$$\frac{dL}{d\beta} = 0 = \frac{1}{\sigma^2} \Sigma \frac{(y_i - \beta x_i)}{x_i^{2\alpha-1}} .$$

Therefore $\hat{\beta} = \dfrac{\Sigma y_i x_i^{1-2\alpha}}{\Sigma x_i^{2-2\alpha}}$.

In the special cases:

	$\alpha = 0$	$\alpha = 1$	$\alpha = \frac{1}{2}$
$\hat{\beta}$	$\dfrac{\Sigma y_i x_i}{\Sigma x_i}$	$\sum \left(\dfrac{y_i}{x_i}\right)$	$\dfrac{\Sigma y_i}{\Sigma x_i}$

The standard error of $\hat{\beta}$ is found using the relationship $V(\hat{\beta}) = 1/I$

$$\frac{d_2 L}{d\beta^2} = -\frac{1}{\sigma^2} \Sigma x_i^{2-2\alpha} .$$

Hence

$$V(\hat{\beta}) = \sigma^2 / \Sigma x_i^{2-2\alpha} .$$

4. The likelihood is

$$\ell = \frac{1}{(2\pi)^{n/2}\sigma^n} \exp\{-\frac{1}{2\sigma^2} (\underline{y} - \underline{a}\underline{\theta})'(\underline{y} - \underline{a}\underline{\theta})\} .$$

Consider

$$(\underline{y} - \underline{a}\underline{\theta})'(\underline{y} - \underline{a}\underline{\theta}) = \underline{y}'\underline{y} - \underline{y}'\underline{a}\underline{\theta} - \underline{\theta}'\underline{a}'\underline{y} + \underline{\theta}'\underline{a}'\underline{a}\underline{\theta} .$$

Hence

$$= \frac{1}{(2\pi)^{n/2}\sigma^n} \exp - \frac{\underline{y}'\underline{y}}{2\sigma^2} \times \exp -\underline{y}'\underline{a}\underline{\theta} - \underline{\theta}'\underline{a}'\underline{y} + \underline{\theta}'\underline{a}'\underline{a}\underline{\theta}) .$$

Hence by the factorisation theorem in Section 3.6 $\underline{a}'\underline{y}$ is sufficient for θ .

EXERCISES 5.2

1. Put

$$\underline{Z}' = (Z_1, Z_2, \ldots, Z_5) \qquad \underline{Y}' = (Y_1, Y_2, \ldots, Y_5)$$

then

$$\underline{Z} = \underline{b}\,\underline{Y}$$

where

$$\underline{b} = \begin{pmatrix} 1 & -1 & 0 & 0 & 0 \\ 1 & 1 & -2 & 0 & 0 \\ 1 & 1 & 1 & -3 & 0 \\ 1 & 1 & 1 & 1 & -4 \\ 1 & 1 & 1 & 1 & 1 \end{pmatrix} .$$

Now

$$\underline{b}\underline{b}' = \begin{matrix} 2 & 0 & 0 & 0 & 0 \\ 0 & 6 & 0 & 0 & 0 \\ 0 & 0 & 12 & 0 & 0 \\ 0 & 0 & 0 & 20 & 0 \\ 0 & 0 & 0 & 0 & 5 \end{matrix} .$$

Hence by (5.12) and since $V(\underline{Y}) = \sigma^2$

$$V(\underline{Z}) = \underline{b}V(\underline{Y})\underline{b}' = \underline{b}\underline{b}'\,\sigma^2 .$$

2. Let $\underline{\theta} = (\theta_1, \theta_2)$
and put

$$\underline{w}' = (x_1, \ldots, x_n, y_1, \ldots, y_n, z_1, \ldots, z_m)$$

then the model is

$$E(\underline{w}) = \underline{a}\,\underline{\theta}$$

where

$$\underline{a} = \begin{pmatrix} 1 & 0 \\ \vdots & \vdots \\ 1 & 0 \\ 0 & 1 \\ \vdots & \vdots \\ 0 & 1 \\ 1 & -1 \\ \vdots & \\ 1 & -1 \end{pmatrix} \begin{matrix} \updownarrow\ n \text{ terms} \\ \\ \updownarrow\ n \text{ terms} \\ \\ \updownarrow\ m \text{ terms} \end{matrix} .$$

Now using the results of least squares theory,

$$\underline{a}'\underline{a} = \begin{pmatrix} n+m & -m \\ -m & n+m \end{pmatrix} \qquad (\underline{a}'\underline{a})^{-1} = (n^2+2mn)^{-1}\begin{pmatrix} n+m & m \\ m & n+m \end{pmatrix}$$

$$\underline{a}'\underline{w} \quad \begin{pmatrix} \sum_{i=1}^{n} x_i + \sum_{i=1}^{m} z_i \\ \sum_{i=1}^{n} y_i - \sum_{i=1}^{m} z_i \end{pmatrix}$$

2. cont'd.

Therefore

$$\underline{\hat{\theta}} = \begin{bmatrix} \dfrac{1}{n(n+2m)} \left[(n+m)\sum_1^n x_i - m\sum_1^n y_i + n\sum_1^m z_i\right] \\ \dfrac{1}{n(n+2m)} \left[m\sum_1^n x_i + (n+m)\sum_1^n y_i - n\sum_1^m z_i\right] \end{bmatrix} .$$

The variance of $(\hat{\theta}_1 - \hat{\theta}_2)$ follows from the result

$$V(\hat{\theta}_1 - \hat{\theta}_2) = V(\hat{\theta}_1) + V(\hat{\theta}_2) - 2C(\hat{\theta}_1, \hat{\theta}_2)$$

and by using $(\underline{a}'\underline{a})^{-1}$.

3. Since we have

$$(\underline{a}'\underline{a}) = \begin{bmatrix} a & 0 & 0 \\ 0 & CS(w,w) & CS(x,w) \\ 0 & CS(x,w) & CS(x,x) \end{bmatrix}$$

the variance matrix is

$$\sigma^2 \begin{bmatrix} \frac{1}{9} & 0 & 0 \\ 0 & \dfrac{CS(x,x)}{\Delta} & -\dfrac{CS(x,w)}{\Delta} \\ 0 & -\dfrac{CS(x,w)}{\Delta} & \dfrac{CS(w,w)}{\Delta} \end{bmatrix}$$

where $\Delta = CS(x,x)\, CS(w,w) - \{CS(x,w)\}^2$.

4. By using (5.12) we have

$$V(\underline{\ell}'\underline{\hat{\theta}}) = \underline{\ell}'V(\underline{\hat{\theta}})\underline{\ell} = \underline{\ell}'\underline{A}^{-1}\underline{\ell}\,\sigma^2$$

and

$$V(\underline{\ell}'\underline{\tilde{\theta}}) = \underline{\ell}'V(\underline{\tilde{\theta}})\underline{\ell} = \underline{\ell}'\underline{dd}'\underline{\ell}\,\sigma^2.$$

Hence if we premultiply (5.21) by $\underline{\ell}'$ and postmultiply by $\underline{\ell}$ the result follows.

EXERCISES 5.3

1. From Theorem 5.3 we have

$$V(\underline{R}) = \underline{m}\,\sigma^2$$

where

$$\underline{m} = \underline{I} - \underline{a}(\underline{a}'\underline{a})^{-1}\underline{a}'.$$

Using the data from Ex.2.3 (§2.6)

$$\underline{a} = \begin{bmatrix} 1 & 0.0509 & 0.0557 \\ 1 & -0.0561 & -0.0393 \\ 1 & 0.0539 & 0.0357 \\ 1 & 0.0089 & 0.0017 \\ 1 & -0.0111 & -0.0083 \\ 1 & -0.0391 & -0.0043 \\ 1 & 0.0379 & 0.0327 \\ 1 & -0.0511 & -0.0723 \\ 1 & 0.0059 & -0.0013 \end{bmatrix}$$

The subsequent evaluation of $V(\underline{R})$, a 9×9 matrix, is straightforward.

EXERCISES 5.4

1. From Theorem 5.6

$$E(S_{par}) = 3\sigma^2 + 9\alpha^2 + \beta_1^2 CS(w,w) + \beta_2^2 CS(x,x) + 2\beta_1\beta_2 CS(x,w) .$$

The sum of squares due to fitting the constant separates as $(\sigma^2 + 9\alpha^2)$. The terms in β_1 and β_2 do not separate unless $CS(x,w)$ is zero.

2. Since the quantity

$$Z = \left(\frac{S_{min}}{\sigma^2}\right)$$

has a χ^2-distribution on $(n-p)$ degrees of freedom, it has a variance of $2(n-p)$. Hence

$$V(\hat{\sigma}^2) = V\left(\frac{\sigma^2 Z}{(n-p)}\right) = \frac{\sigma^4}{(n-p)^2} 2(n-p) = \frac{2\sigma^4}{(n-p)} .$$

EXERCISES 5.5

1. An estimate of $V(\hat{\sigma}^2)$ is

$$\frac{2\hat{\sigma}^4}{27} = \frac{2\,(4.99)^2}{27} = 1.844.$$

2. The basic results needed for this exercise are given towards the end of Chapter 2. Use of those calculations leads to an analysis of variance table as follows:

Source	CSS	d.f.	Mean Square
Regression on w and x	0.05907	2	0.02953
Deviations	0.01023	6	0.00171
Total	0.06930	8	

The F-test is carried out by referring $\frac{0.02953}{0.00171}$ to F-tables on (2,6) degrees of freedom. It will be found that the ratio is clearly significant at the 1% level.

3. As indicated in the question, this is simply a matter of producing sets of points which are symmetrical about their centroid. Any such set of points is acceptable.

4. It would be a mistake to use all the data in obtaining the regression equation. Examination reveals that observations 3, 4 and 5 were taken under special conditions when the high pressure plant was entirely or virtually stopped; it would be better to treat these conditions as a separate case. The last observation is also clearly outside the normal pattern and in a real situation should be checked to see if it is a recording error (H = 379,908 would be more reasonable).

For the purpose of this exercise we will omit these observations to obtain more accurate estimates for use under normal conditions (i.e. $14 \le x_1 \le 20$ and $1 \le x_2 \le 5$). Extrapolation beyond these limits is

4. cont'd.

not justified by a model based on the data provided.

If: y = heat consumed

x_1 = high pressure units

x_2 = low pressure units

then, excluding observations 3, 4 5 and 12:

$\Sigma y = 2{,}385.311 \quad \Sigma x_1 = 134.78 \quad \Sigma x_2 = 22.12$

$\Sigma y^2 = 728{,}846.307 \quad \Sigma x_1^2 = 2285.3775 \quad \Sigma x_2^2 = 80.0714$

$\Sigma yx_1 = 40564.9761 \quad \Sigma yx_2 = 7156.6909$

$\Sigma x_1 x_2 = 382.5213$

$\bar{y} = 298.1639 \quad \bar{x}_1 = 16.8475 \quad \bar{x}_2 = 2.7652$

$CS(y,y) = 17{,}632.7362 \quad CS(x_1,x_2) = 12.6714 \quad CS(x_2,x_2) = 19.2343$

$CS(y,x_1) = 378.4490 \quad CS(y,x_2) = 560.7096$

$CS(x_1,x_2) = 9.8209$

$$\Delta = CS(x_1,x_1)\, CS(x_2,x_2) - CS(x_1,x_2)^2 = 147.2763$$

$$\hat{\beta}_o = \bar{y} = 298.16.$$

$$\hat{\beta}_1 = [CS(y,x_1)\, CS(x_2,x_2) - CS(y,x_2)\, CS(x_1,x_2)]/\Delta = 12.03$$

$$\hat{\beta}_2 = [CS(y,x_2)\, CS(x_1,x_2) - CS(y,x_1)\, CS(x_1,x_2)]/\Delta = 23.01\ .$$

The fitted regression line is therefore

$$\hat{y} = 298.16 + 12.03(x_1-16.85) + 23.01(x_2-2.76)$$

$$\Rightarrow \hat{y} = 31.78 + 12.03x_1 + 23.01x_2\ .$$

5. For the m observations at $t = 0$,

$$E(Y) = \theta_1 + \theta_2\ .$$

For the m observations at $t = t'$,

$$E(Y) = \theta_1 \cos t' + \theta_2 \cos 2t'\ .$$

In matrix form:

$$E(\underset{\sim}{Y}) = \begin{pmatrix} 1 & 1 \\ \vdots & \vdots \\ 1 & 1 \\ \cos t' & \cos 2t' \\ \vdots & \vdots \\ \cos t' & \cos 2t' \end{pmatrix} \begin{pmatrix} \theta_1 \\ \theta_2 \end{pmatrix} \quad \begin{matrix} \updownarrow\ m \text{ rows} \\ \\ \updownarrow\ m \text{ rows} \end{matrix}$$

5. cont'd.

$$\therefore \quad a'a = m\begin{bmatrix} 1+\cos^2 t' & 1+\cos t' \cos 2t' \\ 1+\cos t'\cos 2t' & 1+\cos^2 2t' \end{bmatrix}.$$

Hence

$$(a'a)^{-1} = \frac{1}{m(\cos t' - \cos 2t')^2}\begin{bmatrix} 1+\cos^2 2t' & -(1+\cos t' \cos 2t') \\ -(1+\cos t'\cos 2t') & 1+\cos^2 t' \end{bmatrix}$$

a) at $t' = 0$ or $2\pi/3$, $\cos t' = \cos 2t'$ and estimates of $\underset{\sim}{\theta}$ have infinite variances;

b) iff $t' = \pi$, $(1 + \cos t' \cos 2t') = 0$ and hence

$$\text{Cov}(\hat{\theta}_1, \hat{\theta}_2) = 0 \quad \text{if} \quad t' = \pi .$$

c) $V(\hat{\theta}_1)$ and $V(\hat{\theta}_2)$ are most easily investigated by evaluating them for various values of t'. It will be found that they are both relatively low (0.50) at $t' = \pi$.

d) In view of the above, $t' = \pi$ would seem to be a good choice, but this is at the other extreme of the possible range. $t' = 2\pi/3$ should be avoided, but using $t' =$ (say) $\pi/2$ may be useful, although any value of t' other than $t' = \pi$ introduces complications in that

$$\text{Cov}(\hat{\theta}_1, \hat{\theta}_2) \neq 0.$$

C H A P T E R   S I X

Multiple Regression: Further Analysis and Interpretation

EXERCISES 6.2

1. From Table 6.4 the separate adjusted sums of squares are:

Due to	x_1	25.81
	x_2	11.19
	x_3	130.67
	x_4	2873.95
		3041.62

This is clearly very different from the sums of squares to to x_1, x_2, x_3 and x_4 together, which is 3429.27.

2. This question follows on from Exc.5.5.2.

	CSS	d.f.
Regression on w, x	0.05907	2
Regression on w (x ignored)	0.05747	1
Due to x(adj. for w)	0.00160	1

From Exc.5.5.2. Deviations Mean Square = 0.00171
$F = 0.00160/0.00171 = 0.93567$ on (1,6) d.f.

	CSS	d.f.
Regression on w, x	0.05907	2
Regression on x(w ignored)	0.05528	1
Due to w(adj. for x)	0.00379	1

$F = 0.00379/0.00171 = 2.21637$ on (1,6) d.f.

Since the 5% point on (1,6) d.f. = 5.99, neither w nor x adds significantly to the regression once the other has been included. It can be seen, however, that w on its own accounts for rather more of the variation than x alone.

3. The reference given, Mendenhall and Ott (1971), provides a full discussion of this data.
The model is

$$E(D) = \beta_o + \beta_1 m + \beta_2 m^2 \qquad \text{where} \begin{cases} D = \text{density} \\ m = \text{meter reading} \end{cases}$$

Application of the least squares technique gives

$$E(D) = -36.4943 + 31.8188m - 6.4553m^2$$

We can apply the approach used in section 6.2 to check whether the term in m^2 is desirable; the resulting F-value of 13.27 on (1,15) d.f. is clearly significant at the 1% level.
A graph of D against m drawn using the full regression equation provides the appropriate calibrating curve.

4.(a) Use is made of the following relationships:

$$\alpha_o = \alpha_o.1 = \alpha_o(x_1+x_2+x_3)$$
$$x_1^2 = x_1(1-x_2-x_3) = x_1-x_1x_2-x_1x_3$$
$$x_2^2 = x_2(1-x_1-x_3) = x_2-x_1x_2-x_2x_3$$
$$x_3^2 = x_3(1-x_1-x_2) = x_3-x_1x_3-x_2x_3 \quad .$$

Making the appropriate substitutions, the model readily reduces to the form

$$E(Y) = \beta_1x_1 + \beta_2x_2 + \beta_3x_3 + \beta_4x_1x_2 + \beta_5x_1x_3 + \beta_6x_2x_3 \quad .$$

(b) The trick in this part of the question is to notice that the model to be fitted has no constant term and so the regression line has to pass through the origin. This in turn implies the use of <u>uncorrected</u> sums of squares.
The regression equation will be found to be

$$E(Y) = 2338.53x_1 + 2433.07x_2 + 2640.35x_3 + 372.83x_1x_2 + 1387.37x_1x_3 + 1976.46x_2x_3 \quad .$$

(c) This section requires an examination of the residuals. This is an important part of any statistical analysis as is stressed in earlier chapters (e.g. 5.3) of the main text.

(d) The calculations for plotting a response surface are straight-forward.

5. We have k anova tables of the form

	d.f.
Due to regression	1
Deviations	(n_r-1)
Total	n_r

and the combined Deviations sum of squares has (Σn_r-k) degrees of freedom.

To fit the common slope we minimise

$$S = \sum_{i=1}^{k} \sum_{j=1}^{n_i} (y_{ij}-\beta x_{ij})^2.$$

This leads to an anova table of the form

	d.f.
Due to regression	1
Deviation	Σn_r-1
Total	Σn_r

By subtracting the two (total) deviations sums of squares we have a sum of squares on $(k-1)$ degrees of freedom for testing the hypothesis of a common slope (see Section 6.1).

EXERCISES 6.3

1. This data is discussed briefly in the text. One way of considering the problem is to investigate the effect of including variables x_2,x_3 and x_4 in the regression after using time as a variable. This is done as outlined in section (6.2).

1. cont'd.

Anova Table 1

Source	CSS	d.f.	Mean Square
Regression on t, x_2, x_3, x_4	710.24	4	177.56
Deviations	4.78	5	0.96
Total	715.02	9	

Anova Table 2

Regression on $t(x_2, x_3, x_4$ ign.)	708.20	1	708.20
Due to x_2, x_3, x_4 (adj. for t)	2.04	3	0.68

$$F = 0.68/0.96 = 0.71 \text{ on } (3,5) \text{ d.f.}$$

Since the 5% value of F on (3,5) d.f. is 5.41, the addition of x_2, x_3, x_4 is clearly not significant once time has been included.

2. The main point to be made here is that the model assumes that all the random variation is in the dependent variable, a situation which clearly does not hold in these two cases. One approach would be to use a model involving functional or structural relationships. A detailed discussion may be found in Kendall, M.G. and Stuart, A.(1967) 'The Advanced Theory of Statistics', Griffin & Co., vol.2 (2nd edn.), Ch.29. An analysis of residuals could be carried out to check other assumptions.

EXERCISES 6.5

1. We make use of the results

$$\hat{\underline{\theta}} = (\underline{a}'\underline{a})^{-1}\underline{a}'\underline{Y} \qquad (5.10)$$

$$V(\underline{b}\,\underline{Y}) = \underline{b}\,V(\underline{Y})\underline{b}'. \qquad (5.12)$$

Hence

$$V(\hat{\underline{\theta}}) = (\underline{a}'\underline{a})^{-1}\underline{a}'\,V(\underline{Y})\,\underline{a}(\underline{a}'\underline{a})^{-1}.$$

But $V(\underline{Y}) = V\sigma^2.$ (6.15)

Therefore

$$V(\hat{\underline{\theta}}) = \sigma^2(\underline{a}'\underline{a})^{-1}\,\underline{a}'\underline{V}\,\underline{a}(\underline{a}'\underline{a})^{-1}.$$

2. From (3.21) and (6.15) the likelihood is

$$\ell = \frac{k}{|\underline{V}|^{\frac{1}{2}}}\exp\{-\tfrac{1}{2}(\underline{Y}-\underline{a}\,\underline{\theta})'\underline{V}^{-1}(\underline{Y}-\underline{a}\,\underline{\theta})\}$$

so that

$$L = C - \tfrac{1}{2}\log|\underline{V}| - \tfrac{1}{2}(\underline{Y}-\underline{a}\,\underline{\theta})'\underline{V}^{-1}(\underline{Y}-\underline{a}\,\underline{\theta}).$$

Hence we maximise L by minimising S, where

$$S = (\underline{Y}-\underline{a}\,\underline{\theta})'\underline{V}^{-1}(\underline{Y}-\underline{a}\,\underline{\theta})$$

$$= \underline{Y}'\underline{V}^{-1}\underline{Y} - \underline{Y}'\underline{V}^{-1}\underline{a}\,\underline{\theta} - \underline{\theta}'\underline{a}'\underline{V}^{-1}\underline{Y} + \underline{\theta}'\underline{a}'\underline{V}^{-1}\underline{a}\,\underline{\theta}.$$

Following the method used in section 5.1 we have

2. cont'd.

$$\frac{dS}{d\theta_j} = -\underline{Y}'\underline{V}^{-1}\underline{a}\,\Delta_j - \Delta_j'\,\underline{a}'\underline{V}^{-1}\underline{Y} + \Delta_j'\underline{a}'\underline{V}^{-1}\underline{a}\,\underline{\theta} + \underline{\theta}'\underline{a}'\underline{V}^{-1}\underline{a}\,\Delta_j\ .$$

The equations to be solved are therefore

$$\underline{a}'\underline{V}^{-1}\underline{a}\,\hat{\underline{\theta}} = \underline{a}'\underline{V}^{-1}\underline{Y}\ .$$

Hence

$$\hat{\underline{\theta}} = (\underline{a}'\underline{V}^{-1}\underline{a})^{-1}\underline{a}'V^{-1}\underline{Y}\ .$$

EXERCISES 6.6

1. $E(Y) = \underline{a}\,\hat{\underline{\theta}}$

$\therefore E(Y) = \underline{a}_o'(\underline{a}'\underline{a})^{-1}\underline{a}'\underline{Y}$ at the new point and

$V\{E(Y)\} = V\{\underline{a}\,\hat{\underline{\theta}}\} = \underline{a}\,V(\hat{\underline{\theta}})\underline{a}'$ using (5.12)

But $V(\hat{\theta}) = (\underline{a}'\underline{a})^{-1}\sigma^2$ (5.13)

$\therefore V\{E(Y)\} = \underline{a}_o'(\underline{a}'\underline{a})^{-1}\underline{a}_o\ \sigma^2$ at the new point.

2. We first obtain a new regression equation for Ex. 5.1, using only the explanatory variables x_1, x_3 and x_4,

$$E(Y) = 19.66 + 0.2217(x_1-\bar{x}_1) - 0.1866(x_3-\bar{x}_3) + 0.1565(x_4-\bar{x}_4).$$

Substituting values for x_1, x_3 and x_4 found in Ex.6.4

$$E(Y) = 35.07.$$

We now have $\sigma^2 = 5.21$ and the variance-covariance matrix of the β_j's is given by

$$\begin{bmatrix} 0.010420 & 0.001069 & 0.000034 \\ 0.001069 & 0.000254 & -0.000028 \\ 0.000034 & -0.000028 & 0.000042 \end{bmatrix}$$

Following the lines of Ex.6.4, a 99% confidence interval is

$$35.07 \pm 2.763\ \surd(0.7263) = (32.72,\ 37.42)$$

where 2.763 is the one-sided 0.5% point for t on 28 degrees of freedom. Comparing this result with Ex.6.4 it can be seen that excluding a variable which does not contribute significantly to the regression appears to reduce the prediction error.

3. The method here is explicitly described in the text after (6.18). The appropriate 99% confidence interval is given by

$$35.0 \pm 2.771\ \surd(1.610 + 4.99) = (27.88,\ 42.12).$$

EXERCISES 6.8

1. The analysis will depend on which set of data is chosen, but should in general follow the lines described in the text. The methods discussed briefly in §2.4 provide a good starting point.

C H A P T E R   S E V E N

Polynomial Regression

EXERCISES 7.1

1. In the general case, suppose that observations are taken at n values of the explanatory variable x.

$$\underline{\Theta}' = (\gamma_0, \gamma\ , \gamma\ )$$

$$\underline{a} = \begin{bmatrix} 1 & x_1 & x_1^2 \\ 1 & x_2 & x_2^2 \\ 1 & x_3 & x_3^2 \\ \vdots & \vdots & \vdots \\ 1 & x_n & x_n^2 \end{bmatrix}$$

where x_i is the ith measurement on the explanatory variable $x (1 \le i \le n)$

$$(\underline{a}'\underline{a}) = \begin{bmatrix} n & \sum x_i & \sum x_i^2 \\ \sum x_i & \sum x_i^2 & \sum x_i^3 \\ \sum x_i^2 & \sum x_i^3 & \sum x_i^4 \end{bmatrix} .$$

In the particular case of Ex.7.3

$$\underline{a} = \begin{bmatrix} 1 & -1 & 1 \\ 1 & 0 & 0 \\ 1 & 1 & 1 \\ 1 & 4 & 16 \end{bmatrix} \qquad (\underline{a}'\underline{a}) = \begin{bmatrix} 4 & 4 & 18 \\ 4 & 18 & 64 \\ 18 & 64 & 258 \end{bmatrix} .$$

EXERCISES 7.3

1. The model we have fitted is

$$E(\underline{Y}) = 272.25 + 16.3(x-1.5) - 11.75(x^2-3x+1)$$

$$E(\underline{Y}) = 236.05 + 51.55x - 11.75x^2$$

where x = (distance-2)/2.

$\therefore$ $E(\underline{Y})$ = 172.75 + 37.525(distance) - 2.9375(distance)^2.

Differentiating and equating to zero

0 = 37.525 - 5.875(distance)

$\therefore$ optimum distance ≃ 6.4 inches .

EXERCISES 7.5

1. Plotting the data on a graph, we find that the resulting curve is "*S*" shaped. A simple polynomial model could be used, but while this might give a fairly accurate representation of the central portion of the curve, it is often possible to improve the estimates in the asymptotic parts of the range by the use of suitable transformations. Chapter 8 of the main text contains a full discussion on the use of transformations.

There are often a number of possible alternative models which can be tried in any particular situation. In the present case, a model which may be found more accurate than the simple polynomial is

$E(\underline{Y}) = \alpha e^{\gamma x}/(1-e^{\gamma x})$, or some development of this.

2. *If the* polynomials are

$$f_1 = x + a$$
$$f_2 = x + bx + c$$

then $\sum f_1 = 0$, which leads to $a = -1\frac{1}{3}$.
Also

$$f_2 = 0 \quad \text{and} \quad \sum f_2 = 0$$

which gives the equations

$$10 + 4b + 3c = 0$$
$$28 + 10b + 4c = 0 .$$

Solving this simultaneously

$$b = -22/7 \quad \text{and} \quad c = 6/7 .$$

Hence

$$f_1 = x - 1\tfrac{1}{3}$$
$$f_2 = (7x^2-22x+6)/7.$$

We can check these:

x	0	1	3
f_1	$-1\frac{1}{3}$	$-\frac{1}{3}$	$1\frac{2}{3}$
f_2	$\frac{6}{7}$	$-\frac{9}{7}$	$\frac{3}{7}$

$\sum f_1 = 0$

$\sum f_2 = 0$

$\sum f_1 f_2 = 0$.

3. | x | −2 | −1 | 0 | 1 | 2 |
|---|---|---|---|---|---|
| *freq.* | 1 | 2 | 3 | 2 | 1 |

The frequencies are symmetrical about zero, hence:

<u>Linear</u> $\quad f_1 = x$

<u>Quadratic</u> $\quad f_2 = x^2 - a$

$$\sum f_2 = 0: \qquad 12-9a = 0, \qquad a = 4/3 \qquad f_2 = x^2 - 4/3.$$

<u>Cubic</u> $\quad f_3 = x^3 - bx$

$$\sum x f_3 = 0: \qquad 36-12b = 0, \qquad b = 3 \qquad f_3 = x - 3x$$

<u>Quartic</u> $\quad f_4 = x^4 + cx^2 + d$

$$\sum f_4 = 0: \qquad 36-12c - 9d = 0$$

$$\sum x^2 f_4 = 0: \qquad 132-36c - 12d = 0\ .$$

These yield

$$\left.\begin{array}{l} 12 - 4c - 3d = 0 \\ 11 - 3c - d = 0 \end{array}\right\} \qquad f_4 = (5x^4 - 21x^2 + 8)/5.$$

Check:

						$\sum f^2$
	−2	−1	0	1	2	12
(÷3)	8	−1	−4	−1	8	180/9 = 20
	−2	2	0	−2	2	24
(÷5)	4	−8	8	−8	4	480/25 = 19.2

Hence polynomial is

$$E(y) = \bar{y} + \hat{\alpha}_1 x + \hat{\alpha}_2 (x^2 - 4/3) + \hat{\alpha}_3 (x^3 - 3x) + \hat{\alpha}_4 (5x^4 - 21x^2 + 8)/5\ .$$

The variance of this is at x'

$$\sigma^2\left\{\frac{1}{9} + \frac{1}{12}x'^2 + \frac{1}{20}(x'^2 - 4/3)^2 + \frac{1}{24}(x'^3 - 3x')^2 + \frac{1}{19.2}(5x'^4 - 21x'^2 + 8)^2\right\}.$$

4. This is a more complicated problem and so will be dealt with in greater detail than the previous questions. What we are interested in here is fitting a quadratic and estimating the position of its maximum, but matters are complicated by the fact that the experiment is in two blocks. The easiest form of model to fit is:

$$E(y|\text{process } 1) = \alpha - \gamma + \beta_1 f_1 + \beta_2 f_2$$

$$E(y|\text{process } 2) = \alpha + \gamma + \beta_1 f_1 + \beta_2 f_2\ .$$

The design matrix is

$$X = \begin{array}{c} \begin{array}{cccc} \alpha & \gamma & \beta_1 & \beta_2 \end{array} \\ \begin{bmatrix} 1 & -1 & -5 & 5 \\ 1 & +1 & -3 & -1 \\ 1 & +1 & -1 & -4 \\ 1 & -1 & 1 & -4 \\ 1 & -1 & 3 & -1 \\ 1 & +1 & 5 & 5 \end{bmatrix} \end{array}$$

4. cont'd.

Hence

$$X'X = \begin{bmatrix} 6 & 0 & 0 & 0 \\ 0 & 6 & 2 & 0 \\ 0 & 2 & 70 & 0 \\ 0 & 0 & 0 & 84 \end{bmatrix} \text{ and } (X'X)^{-1} = \begin{bmatrix} \frac{1}{6} & 0 & 0 & 0 \\ 0 & \frac{70}{416} & -\frac{2}{416} & 0 \\ 0 & -\frac{2}{416} & \frac{6}{416} & 0 \\ 0 & 0 & 0 & \frac{1}{84} \end{bmatrix}$$

Also

$$X'\underline{Y} = \begin{bmatrix} 44.95 \\ -7.07 \\ 15.45 \\ -27.73 \end{bmatrix}$$

$\hat{\alpha} = 7.492$ (std. error = 0.408)

$\hat{\gamma} = -1.264$ (std. error = 0.410)

$\hat{\beta}_1 = 0.257$ (std. error = 0.120)

$\hat{\beta}_2 = -0.330$ (std. error = 0.109)

(Note: The standard errors are the square roots of the diagonal elements of $(X'X)^{-1}$, since the question tells us we may assume $\sigma^2 = 1$. Also we note in the estimates of $\hat{\gamma}$ and $\hat{\beta}_2$ significant evidence, respectively, of process effect and of the need for a quadratic term.)

In order to estimate the time delay for maximum yield, we have to know the form of the polynomials f_1 and f_2. They are, with $x = (\text{day}-3.5)$,

$$f_1 = 2x \quad \text{and} \quad f_2 = 3/2(x^2-35/12).$$

Thus

$$\frac{d}{dx}[\beta_1 f_1 + \beta_2 f_2] = 2\beta_1 + 3\beta_2 x .$$

Equating this to zero and solving, we see that the maximum yield (if $\beta_2 < 0$) is obtained if

$x = -\dfrac{2\beta_1}{3\beta_2}$. Substituting our estimates of β_1 and β_2,

$x = 0.519$ (i.e. day = 4.019).

For a confidence interval for $\dfrac{2\beta_1}{3\beta_2}$ we take the set of all x values such that the null hypothesis

$\dfrac{2\beta_1}{3\beta_2} = -x$ would not be rejected. We therefore have to find (for a 95% confidence interval) the set of all x values such that

$$\frac{|2\hat{\beta}_1 + 3x\hat{\beta}_2|}{\sqrt{(4 \operatorname{var}\hat{\beta}_1 + 9x^2 \operatorname{var}\hat{\beta}_2)}} \leq 1.96 .$$

Substituting numerical values and solving the quadratic, the confidence interval is given by

$x = (0.043, 1.746)$

i.e. a 95% confidence interval for the time delay corresponding to maximum yield extends from 3.5 days to 5.2 days.

CHAPTER EIGHT

The use of transformations

EXERCISES 8.4

1. Plotting log W against R for the data given in Table 8.1 gives a nearly straight line. The model (8.3) is therefore clearly reasonable for use with this data, although with other sets of data one must bear in mind warnings given previously in the text concerning the use of a model beyond the limits of the data set from which it is derived.

The text discussion of this data emphasises that the original data has been modified to exclude zero and negative values of the weight loss. If there are such values, one is forced to use a more complicated model, possibly of the form

$$E(Y) = \alpha + \beta e^{\alpha x} .$$

EXERCISES 8.5

1. A good discussion of the problems concerning the two-parameter family of transformations is given in the original paper by Box and Cox (1964), and in the discussion following the paper. It is better if there is some external reason for setting λ_2 , so that the likeli hood is only maximised for λ_1 .

2. The result is that an approximate 95% confidence interval for λ is (0.5,0.9). The value 0.5 is considerably better than 1.0, but the maximum likelihood estimate is $\lambda = 0.7$.

EXERCISES 8.6

1. A discussion of the use of a quadratic function with the Box-Tidwell procedure is given on p.537 of the original paper by Box and Tidwell (1962).

CHAPTER NINE

Correlation

EXERCISES 9.2

1. Since a variance is positive

$$V(X+Y) \geq 0$$

$$V(X) + 2C(X,Y) + V(Y) \geq 0 \ .$$

But $V(X) = V(Y) = 1$ and $C(X,Y) = \rho$ so that

$$\rho \geq -1 \ .$$

Similarly we use

$$V(X-Y) \geq 0$$

to obtain

$$\rho \leq 1 \ .$$

EXERCISES 9.3

1. From Exc.4.4.3 we can derive the following equation

$$\frac{d^2L}{d\rho^2} = \frac{n(1+\rho^2)}{(1-\rho^2)^2} - \frac{(1+3\rho^2)}{(1-\rho^2)^3}\sum(x_i^2 - 2\rho x_i y_i + y_i) + \frac{4\rho}{(1-\rho^2)^2}\sum x_i y_i \ .$$

Since $E(x_i^2) = E(y_i^2) = 1$ and $E(x_i y_i) = \rho$ we have

$$E\left[\frac{d^2L}{d\rho^2}\right] = \frac{n(1+\rho^2)}{(1-\rho^2)^2} - \frac{(1+3\rho^2)}{(1-\rho^2)^3}\,(2n - 2\rho^2) + \frac{4n\rho^2}{(1-\rho^2)^2}$$

$$= -\frac{n(1+\rho^2)}{(1-\rho^2)^2}$$

and so, from Theorem 4.2, the asymptotic variance of the estimator is

$$\text{Var}(\hat{\rho}) = -1/E\,\frac{d^2L}{d\rho^2} = \frac{(1-\rho^2)^2}{n(1+\rho^2)} \ .$$

EXERCISES 9.4

1. If we assume that

$$E(R) = \rho$$

then we require a function $f(\rho)$ with

$$f'(\rho)\sigma(\rho) = c,$$

a constant. Now, asymptotically

$$V(R) = \frac{(1-\rho^2)^2}{(n\ 1)}$$

$$= \sigma^2(\rho)$$

so that

$$f'(\rho) = \frac{d}{(1-\rho^2)}$$

where $d = (n-1)c$.
Putting $d = 1$ and integrating gives Fisher's Z-transformation

$$Z = \tfrac{1}{2} \log_e \{(1+R)/(1-R)\} .$$

EXERCISES 9.5

1. Using Fisher's Z-transformation we have

$$\zeta(0.5) = \tfrac{1}{2} \log_e 3 + \frac{0.5}{2.1400} = 0.549$$

so that

$$\zeta(\rho_o) + 1.96 \frac{1}{\sqrt{n-3}} = 0.576$$

Thus the observed Z value of 0.623 is significantly different from 0.5.

Some 90% confidence intervals for the correlation coefficient can be obtained by solving

$$\zeta(r) = 0.553 \pm 1.645/\sqrt{1398} .$$

The right hand side gives (0.526, 0.580). Since n is large we can i nore the correction term of $O(\frac{1}{n})$ in $\zeta(\rho)$ and use transformation tables to give a 90% confidence interval for ρ of 0.481,0.521).

2. For testing the hypothesis $\rho = 0$ the upper 95% significance points for various n using (9.19), (9.21) and Table 13 of Pearson and Hartley are given in columns (1), (2) and (3) respectively of the following table.

95% significance points for testing hypotheses $\rho = 0$.

n	(1)	(2)	(3)
100	0.197	0.197	0.197
50	0.280	0.278	0.275
35	0.336	0.333	0.335
25	0.400	0.395	0.398
20	0.450	0.442	0.444
15	0.524	0.512	0.514
10	0.653	0.630	0.632
8	0.741	0.704	0.707
6	0.877	0.812	0.811
5	0.980	0.882	0.878
4	1.132	0.961	0.950

2. cont'd.

Generally the exact values and those given by (9.21) are in good agreement. However for small sample sizes (9.19) gives a rather wide acceptance interval, including upper limits greater than one for $n = 2, 3, 4$.

3. The value of the test statistic (9.26) given by the observed correlations is

$$\frac{0.829 - 0.604}{\sqrt{2/47}} = 1.09$$

which is clearly not significant.

CHAPTER TEN

The Analysis of Variance

EXERCISES 10.1

1. Since $\gamma_4 = -(\gamma_1 + \gamma_2 + \gamma_3)$ we have

$$\underline{b} = \begin{pmatrix} 1 & 1 & 0 & 0 \\ 1 & 1 & 0 & 0 \\ 1 & 1 & 0 & 0 \\ 1 & 0 & 1 & 0 \\ 1 & 0 & 1 & 0 \\ 1 & 0 & 1 & 0 \\ 1 & 0 & 0 & 1 \\ 1 & 0 & 0 & 1 \\ 1 & 0 & 0 & 1 \\ 1 & -1 & -1 & -1 \\ 1 & -1 & -1 & -1 \\ 1 & -1 & -1 & -1 \end{pmatrix}.$$

The results follow easily.

EXERCISES 10.2

1. Multiplying (10.17) by $\underline{A}$ gives

$$\underline{A}\,\underline{X} = \underline{A}\,\underline{A}^{-}\underline{Y} + \underline{A}(\underline{A}^{-}\underline{A} - \underline{I})\underline{W}$$
$$= \underline{A}\,\underline{A}^{-}\underline{Y}$$

and since $\underline{A}^{-}\underline{Y}$ is a solution of (10.15) so is (10.17).

2. Let $\underline{\tilde{X}}$ be any solution of (10.15) and so

$$\underline{A}^{-}\underline{A}\,\underline{\tilde{X}} = \underline{A}^{-}\underline{Y}.$$

Now putting

$$\underline{W} = (\underline{A}^{-}\underline{A} - \underline{I})\underline{\tilde{X}}$$

and substituting into (10.17) gives

$$\underline{A}^{-}\underline{Y} + (\underline{A}^{-}\underline{A} - \underline{I})\underline{W} = \underline{A}^{-}\underline{Y} + (\underline{A}^{-}\underline{A}\,\underline{A}^{-}\underline{A} - 2\,\underline{A}^{-}\underline{A} + \underline{I})\underline{\tilde{X}}$$
$$= \underline{A}^{-}\underline{Y} + (I - AA^{-})\underline{\tilde{X}}$$
$$= \underline{\tilde{X}}$$

EXERCISES 10.3

1. From (10.31)

$$\underline{R} = \underline{Y} - \underline{a}\,\underline{A}^{-}\underline{a}'\underline{Y}$$
$$= (I - P)\underline{Y}$$

so that

$$E(\underline{R}) = (\underline{I} - \underline{a}\,\underline{A}^{-}\underline{a}')E(\underline{Y})$$
$$= (\underline{a} - \underline{a}\,\underline{A}^{-}\underline{a}'\underline{a})\underline{\theta}$$
$$= \underline{0}$$

since $\underline{a}\,\underline{A}^{-}\underline{a}'\underline{a} = \underline{a}$.

As P is symmetric and $\underline{P}\,\underline{P} = \underline{P}$ we observe that

$$(I - P)(\underline{I} - \underline{P})' = \underline{I} - 2\underline{P} + \underline{P}\,\underline{P}$$
$$= \underline{I} - \underline{P} \;.$$

Hence

$$V(\underline{R}) = (\underline{I} - \underline{P})\sigma^2\,(\underline{I} - \underline{P})'$$
$$= (\underline{I} - \underline{P})\sigma^2.$$

2. $C(\underline{R}, \underline{\theta}) = C((\underline{I} - \underline{P})\underline{Y}, \underline{A}^{-}\underline{a}'\underline{Y})$

$$= (\underline{I} - \underline{P})C(\underline{Y},\underline{Y})\underline{a}\,\underline{A}^{-}$$
$$= (\underline{I} - \underline{P})\,\underline{I}\sigma^2\underline{a}\,\underline{A}^{-}$$
$$= \sigma^2(\underline{a}\,\underline{A}^{-} - \underline{a}\,\underline{A}^{-}\underline{a}'\underline{a}\,\underline{A}^{-})$$
$$= \sigma^2(\underline{a}\,\underline{A}^{-} - \underline{a}\,\underline{A}^{-})$$
$$= \underline{0}$$

as required.

To prove (10.33) we firstly need to show that

$$\mathrm{tr}(\underline{A}^{-}\underline{A}) = \mathrm{rank}(\underline{a})$$
$$= p$$

for any A^{-}. However, from (10.23), for any generalised inverses $\underline{A}_1^{-}$ and $\underline{A}_2^{-}$ of $\underline{A}$

$$\mathrm{tr}(\underline{a}\,\underline{A}_1^{-}\underline{a}') = \mathrm{tr}(\underline{a}\,\underline{A}_2^{-}\underline{a}')$$

and so

$$\mathrm{tr}(\underline{A}_1^{-}\underline{a}'\underline{a}) = \mathrm{tr}(\underline{A}_2^{-}\underline{a}'\underline{a})$$

2. cont'd.

that is

$$\mathrm{tr}(\underline{A}_1^- \underline{A}) = \mathrm{tr}(\underline{A}_2^- \underline{A}) .$$

So it is only necessary to prove the result for a particular $\underline{A}^-$.

Now a suitable choice of the matrix $\underline{B}$ in the method of construction of a generalised inverse is the matrix whose columns are the orthonormal latent vectors of $\underline{A}$. Then

$$\underline{B}'\underline{B} = \underline{B}\,\underline{B}' = \underline{I}$$

and $\underline{D}$ is the diagonal matrix of latent roots of $\underline{A}$ of which exactly p are non-zero. Then since

$$\underline{A} = \underline{B}^{-1}\underline{B}\,\underline{B}'^{-1} = \underline{B}'\underline{D}\,\underline{B}$$

and

$$\underline{A}^- = \underline{B}'\underline{D}^-\underline{B} = \underline{B}'\underline{D}^-\,\underline{B}$$

we have

$$\begin{aligned}\mathrm{tr}(\underline{A}^-\underline{A}) &= \mathrm{tr}(\underline{B}'\underline{D}^-\underline{B}\,\underline{B}'\underline{D}\,\underline{B}) \\ &= \mathrm{tr}(\underline{D}^-\underline{D}\,\underline{B}\,\underline{B}') \\ &= \mathrm{tr}(\underline{D}^-\underline{D}) \\ &= p\end{aligned}$$

as required.

Hence

$$\begin{aligned}E(S_{\mathrm{min}}) &= E(\underline{R}'\underline{R}) \\ &= \mathrm{tr}\ E(\underline{R}'\underline{R}) \\ &= \mathrm{tr}\ E(\underline{R}\,\underline{R}') \\ &= \mathrm{tr}\ V(\underline{R}) \\ &= \mathrm{tr}(\underline{I}-\underline{P})\sigma^2 \\ &= \sigma^2\ \mathrm{tr}\ \underline{I} - \sigma^2\ \mathrm{tr}(\underline{a}'\underline{a}\,\underline{A}^-) \\ &= \sigma^2(n-p) .\end{aligned}$$

Lastly

$$\begin{aligned}E(S_{\mathrm{par}}) &= E(\hat{\underline{\theta}}'\underline{a}'\underline{a}\,\hat{\underline{\theta}}) = \mathrm{tr}\ E(\hat{\underline{\theta}}\,\underline{a}'\underline{a}\,\hat{\underline{\theta}}) \\ &= \mathrm{tr}\ E(\underline{a}\,\hat{\underline{\theta}}\,\underline{\theta}'\underline{a}') \\ &= \mathrm{tr}\ \underline{a}\{V(\hat{\underline{\theta}}) + E(\hat{\underline{\theta}})\,E(\hat{\underline{\theta}}')\}\underline{a}' \\ &= \mathrm{tr}\{\sigma^2\underline{a}\,\underline{A}^-\underline{a}' + \underline{a}\,\underline{\theta}\,\underline{\theta}'\underline{a}'\} \\ &= \sigma^2\ \mathrm{tr}(\underline{A}\,\underline{A}^-) + \mathrm{tr}(\underline{\theta}'\underline{a}'\underline{a}\,\underline{\theta}) \\ &= p\,\sigma^2 + \underline{\theta}'\underline{a}'\underline{a}\,\underline{\theta}\end{aligned}$$

as required.

EXERCISES 10.4

1. The total corrected sum of squares is

$$\sum_{i=1}^{t}\sum_{j=1}^{r}(y_{ij}-\bar{y}_{..})^2 = \sum\sum\{(y_{ij}-\bar{y}_{i.}) + (\bar{y}_{i.}-\bar{y}_{..})\}^2$$

$$= \sum\sum(y_{ij}-\bar{y}_{i.})^2 + \sum\sum(\bar{y}_{i.}-\bar{y}_{..})^2 + 2\sum\sum(y_{ij}-\bar{y}_{i.})(\bar{y}_{i.}-\bar{y}_{..})$$

$$= \sum\sum(y_{ij}-\bar{y}_{i.})^2 + r(\bar{y}_{i.} \; -\bar{y}_{..})^2 \; ,$$

as required.

2.(a) For model (1)

$$\underline{a} = \underline{1}$$

and

$$\underline{\Theta} = \{\mu\} \; .$$

So, by Theorem 5.6, if p is the number of treatments then

$$E(S_{\text{par}}^{(1)}) = p\,\sigma^2 + \underline{\Theta}'\underline{a}'\underline{a}\,\underline{\Theta}$$

$$= \sigma^2 + r\,t\,\mu^2 \quad .$$

For model (2)

$$\underline{a} = \begin{pmatrix} 1 & 0 & 0 & \\ 1 & \cdot & \cdot & \cdots \\ \vdots & \vdots & \vdots & \\ 1 & 0 & \cdot & \\ 0 & 1 & \cdot & \\ \cdot & 1 & \cdot & \cdots \\ \vdots & \vdots & \vdots & \\ \cdot & 1 & 0 & \\ \cdot & 0 & 1 & \\ \cdot & \cdot & 1 & \cdots \\ \vdots & \vdots & \vdots & \\ \cdot & \cdot & 1 & \\ \cdot & \cdot & 0 & \cdots \\ \vdots & \vdots & \vdots & \\ 0 & 0 & 0 & \end{pmatrix} \quad \begin{matrix} \updownarrow r \\ \updownarrow r \\ \\ t \text{ set of } r \text{ rows as shown} \end{matrix}$$

$\longleftarrow t$ columns $\longrightarrow$

and

$$\underline{\Theta} = (\gamma_1, \gamma_2, \ldots, \gamma\;),$$

since $\mu = \sum_{i=1}^{t}\gamma_i$.

Thus, again using Theorem 5.6

$$E(S_{\text{par}}^{(2)}) = t\,\sigma^2 + r\sum_{i=1}^{t}\gamma_i^2$$

and hence the expected mean square due to treatments is

$$E(MS_T) = E\left\{\frac{1}{t-1}\,(S_{\text{par}}^{(2)} - S_{\text{par}}^{(1)})\right\}$$

2. cont'd.

$$= \sigma^2 + \frac{r}{t-1} \sum (\gamma_i - \bar{\gamma}_.)^2 \quad .$$

(b) Firstly we note that

$$\bar{Y}_{i.} = \mu + \gamma_i + \bar{\varepsilon}_{i.}$$
$$\bar{Y}_{..} = \mu + \bar{\gamma}_. + \bar{\varepsilon}_{..}$$

$$E(\varepsilon_{ij}) = 0$$

and $E(\varepsilon_{ij}\varepsilon_{k\ell}) = \begin{cases} 0 & \text{if } i \neq k \text{ or } j \neq \ell \\ \sigma^2 & \text{if } i = k \text{ and } j = \ell, \end{cases}$

since $V(\underline{Y}) = \sigma^2\underline{I}$, for all $i,k = 1,2,\ldots, t$ and $j,\ell = 1, 2, \ldots, r$..

So the expected treatment sum of squares is

$$E\left\{r \sum_{i=1}^{t} (\bar{y}_{i.} - \bar{y}_{..})^2\right\} = r \sum_{i=1}^{t} E(\gamma_i - \bar{\gamma}_. + \bar{\varepsilon}_{i.} - \bar{\varepsilon}_{..})^2$$

$$= r\sum(\gamma_i-\bar{\gamma}_.)^2 + r\sum(\gamma_i-\bar{\gamma}_.)E(\bar{\varepsilon}_i - \bar{\varepsilon}_{..}) + r\sum E(\bar{\varepsilon}_{i.}^2 + \bar{\varepsilon}_{..}^2 - 2\bar{\varepsilon}_{i.}\bar{\varepsilon}_{..})$$
$$= r\sum(\gamma_i-\bar{\gamma}_.)^2 + 0 + r\sum\sigma^2\left(\frac{1}{r} + \frac{1}{rt} - \frac{2}{rt}\right)$$
$$= r\sum(\gamma_i-\bar{\gamma}_.)^2 + \sigma^2(t-1) \; .$$

Dividing the expected treatment sum of squares by $(t-1)$ gives the required result.

3. Following the argument under table 10.1 the expected residual sum of squares is seen to be, using the results given in question 2 above,

$$E\left\{\sum_{i=1}^{t}\sum_{j=1}^{r} (y_{ij} - \bar{y}_{i.})^2\right\} = \sum\sum E(\varepsilon_{ij} - \bar{\varepsilon}_{i.})^2$$
$$= \sum\sum E(\varepsilon_{ij}^2 - \bar{\varepsilon}_{i.}^2 - 2\varepsilon_{ij}\bar{\varepsilon}_{i.})$$
$$= \sum\sum\sigma^2\left(1 + \frac{1}{r} - \frac{2}{r}\right)$$
$$= \sigma^2 t(r-1).$$

Thus the expected residual mean square is σ^2 .

EXERCISES 10.5

1. The two-tailed 1% significance level for the t-distribution on 8 degrees of freedom is 3.26. Thus the *LSD* at 1% for Ex.10.1 is

$$3.26 \times 1.36 = 4.43 \; .$$

2. The variance of the difference between $\bar{y}_C$ and $(\bar{y}_A+\bar{y}_B+\bar{y}_D)/3$ is $\frac{4}{3}\frac{\sigma^2}{r}$ so that the *LSD* at 5% for this difference is $t_\nu(5\%)2s/\sqrt{3r}$ where s^2 is the residual mean square and ν is the number of degrees of freedom for s^2. For Ex.10.1 this gives

$$2.31 \times 1.11 = 2.56 \; .$$

2 cont'd.

If this comparison was considered to be of interest before the analysis was done then this is an exact t-test. However if it was performed as a result of the previous *LSD* analysis then this test is conditional on the results of the previous test.

3. This subject matter is dealt with in chapter 6 and also, for example, Chaterjee and Price (1977).**

EXERCISES 10.7

1. The analysis of the residuals is a practical question involving the drawing of graphs and will be left to the reader.

It can easily be shown that the variances and covariances of the residuals are given by

$$V(R_{ij}) = \frac{(t-1)(b-1)}{tb}\sigma^2$$

$$C(R_{ij},R_{hj}) = -(\frac{b-1}{tb})\sigma^2 \quad \text{for} \quad j \neq k$$

$$C(R_{ij},R_{hj}) = -(\frac{b-1}{tb})\sigma^2 \quad \text{for} \quad i \neq h$$

$$C(R_{ij},R_{hk}) = \frac{1}{tb}\sigma^2 \quad \text{for} \quad i \neq h, \; j \neq k$$

so that the correlations are

$$\rho(R_{ij},R_{ik}) = -\frac{1}{(t-1)} \quad \text{for} \quad j \neq k$$

$$\rho(R_{ij},R_{hj}) = -\frac{1}{(t-1)} \quad \text{for} \quad i \neq h$$

$$\rho(R_{ij},R_{hk}) = \frac{1}{(t-1)(b-1)} \quad \text{for} \quad i \neq h, \; j \neq k$$

for $i, h = 1, 2, \ldots, t$ and $j, k = 1, 2, \ldots, b$.
For Ex.10.2 $t = b = 3$ so the correlations are

$$\rho(R_{ij},R_{hk}) = \begin{cases} \frac{1}{4} & \text{for } i \neq h, \; j \neq k \\ -\frac{1}{2} & \text{for either } i \neq h \text{ or } j \neq k . \end{cases}$$

These correlations are quite large.

2. This is a practical question and will not be dealt with here.

3. Let y_{ij} be the observation in the ith group on the jth chick. Then the model to be fitted is

$$y_{ij} = \mu + \beta_i + \gamma_j + \varepsilon_{ij}$$

$i = 1, 2, \ldots, 8$; $j = 1, 2, 3$, where ε_{ij} represents error, with $E(\varepsilon_{ij}) = 0$ and $V(\varepsilon_{ij}) = \sigma^2$.

This is the form of the model for a two-way analysis of variance.

3. cont'd.

Table of Sums of Squares

Sum of Squares	Total	Donor	Group
U.S.S.	1550.30	1516.32	1465.42
Correction	1435.31	1435.31	1435.31
C.S.S	114.99	81.01	30.11

This gives the following analysis of variance table.

Anova Table

Source	C.S.S.	D.F.	M.S.	F
Between Group	30.11	7	4.30	16.17
Between Donor	81.01	2	40.50	152.25
Residual	3.87	14	0.266	
Total	114.99	23		

The F-value for between donor is clearly very highly significant so we conclude that there is real evidence of a difference in the percentage increase of lymphocytes in the blood of Barred Columbian chicks between the donors.

The donor means are:

Donor	Mean
Barred Columbian	6.1
R.I.R. B.C.	6.8
Rhode Island Red	10.3

and the variance of a donor mean is $\frac{1}{4}\sigma^2$. So the least significance difference (LSD) at 5% is

$$t_{14}(5\%) \times s/2 = 2.15 \times 0.258$$
$$= 0.56 \,.$$

This suggests that there is a difference between the Rhode Island Red donor and the remaining two donors, and that there may also be a difference between the Barred Columbian and R.I.R. B.C. donors although this difference is not as marked.

The $F(2,14)$ 1% point is 6.15 and so we conclude that there is very strong evidence of a difference between groups. The variance of a group mean is $2/3\,\sigma^2$ and this gives a LSD at 5% of

$$2.15 \times 0.421 = 0.91.$$

This can now be used to examine where the group differences lie.

It is noted here that one could have taken logarithms of the percentage increases to create a truly additive model but that in this case it causes little change in the results.

4. Since we must assume a fixed probability for each treatment of reaching mid-mitosis in the fixed time interval, it is likely that the data follows a binomial distribution and hence (see chapter 8) a transformation of the form

4. cont'd.

$$\sin^{-1}\sqrt{\frac{r}{n}}$$

is necessary to transform to normalized probabilities and then a randomised block analysis can be used.

Table of Transformed Data

	Group			
Experiment	Control	X-ray	Beta	Totals
1	.831	.421	.524	1.776
2	1.137	.615	.685	2.437
3	.735	.497	.330	1.562
4	1.240	.539	.633	2.412
Totals	3.943	2.072	2.172	8.187

Table of Sums of Squares

Sum of Squares	Total	Group	Experiment
U.S.S.	6.4075	6.1395	5.7836
Correction	5.5856	5.5856	5.5856
C.S.S.	0.8219	0.5539	0.1980

This gives the following analysis of variance table

Source	C.S.S.	d.F.	M.S.	F
Experiment	0.1980	3	0.066	5.641
Group	0.5539	2	0.277	23.675
Residuals	0.0700	6	0.0117	
Total	0.8219	11		

Since the 1% point of $F(2,6)$ is 10.92 we conclude that there is very strong evidence of a difference between the proportions of cells reaching mid-mitosis. The 5% point of $F(3,6)$ is 4.76 and so we see that the sum of squares due to experiment is just significant.

Table of Group Means

Group	Control	X-ray	Beta
Mean	0.986	0.518	0.543

The *LSD* at 5% for a difference of group means is

$$t_6(5\%)\, s\sqrt{2/3} \;=\; 2.45 \times \sqrt{0.0117 \times 2/3}$$
$$= 0.216\ .$$

4. cont'd.

We conclude that irradiation has a marked effect on the proportion of cells reaching mid-mitosis but that there is no appreciable difference in the effects of X-ray and Beta radiation.

The *LSD* at 5% for the difference between two experiments' means is 0.187 and this could be used to examine where any differences between the four experiments exist.

One problem with using the transformation

$$Z_i = \sin^{-1}\sqrt{r_i/n_i}$$

with the n_i not all equal is that the transformed data will have non-constant variance since

$$V(Z_i) \approx 1/(4n_i) .$$

However, since there are approximately equal observations for each experiment this should not have too great an effect.

This problem could have also been dealt with by using a log transformation or using generalised linear models (see chapter 17).

EXERCISES 10.8

1. The model is

$$Y_{ij} = \mu + \alpha_i + \varepsilon_{ij} \quad \begin{cases} i = 1, 2, \ldots, t \\ j = 1, 2, \ldots, n_i \end{cases} ,$$

with $\varepsilon_{ij} \sim N(0,\sigma^2)$.

We require to minimise the sum of squares

$$S = \sum_{i=1}^{t} \sum_{j=1}^{n_i} (y_{ij} - \mu - \alpha_i)^2$$

from which we have

$$\frac{\partial S}{\partial \mu} = -2 \sum_i \sum_j (y_{ij} - \mu - \alpha_i)$$

and

$$\frac{\partial S}{\partial \alpha_i} = -2 \sum_j (y_{ij} - \mu - \alpha_i) , \qquad i = 1, 2, \ldots, t .$$

The normal equations are

$$\bar{y}_{..} = \hat{\mu} + (\sum_i n_i \hat{\alpha}_i)/(\sum n_i)$$

$$\bar{y}_{i.} = \hat{\mu} + \hat{\alpha}_i .$$

Hence, once again the residuals are defined by

$$y_{ij} - \hat{\mu} - \hat{\alpha}_i = y_{ij} - \bar{y}_{i.}$$

giving the minimised sum of squares to be

$$\sum_i \sum_j (y_{ij} - \hat{\mu} - \hat{\alpha}_i)^2 = \sum_i \sum_j (y_{ij} - \bar{y}_{i.})^2 .$$

Subtracting the residual sum of squares from the total corrected sum of squares gives the sum of squares of the fitted values to be

1. cont'd.

$\sum_i n_i(\bar{y}_{i.} - \bar{y}_{..})^2$. The analysis of variance table then follows easily.

The expected error and treatment mean squares are

$$E(M.S._\epsilon) = \sigma^2$$

and

$$E(M.S._\tau) = \sigma^2 + \frac{1}{t-1}\sum_{i=1}^{t} n_i \alpha_i^2$$

respectively.

**

Reference (Exercises 10.5.3.)

Chaterjee, S. and Price, B. (1977) 'Regression analysis by example'. J. Wiley, New York.

C H A P T E R   E L E V E N

Designs with regressions in the treatment effects

EXERCISES 11.1

1. A logarithmic transformation yields the following data:

Time(mins)	6	18	30	42	54
	3.401	2.186	1.411	0.588	-0.223
	3.353	2.079	1.526	0.956	-0.511
	3.350	2.380	1.548	0.788	0.000
Mean	3.368	2.215	1.495	0.777	-0.245

Overall mean = 1.522 Correction = 34.7533 .

Since the times are equally spaced, we can use orthogonal polynomials for the regression. The new x_i are -2,-1,0,1,2, and the corrected sum of products is

$$CS(\bar{y},x\ ) = (-2\times 3.368\ \ -1\times 2.215 + 0\times 1.495 + 1\times 0.777\ \ -2\times 0.245)$$

$$CS(x,\ x) = (-2)^2 + (-1)^2 + (0)^2 + (1)^2 + (2)^2 = 10.$$

Then the sum of squares attributable to the regression is, since there are three replicates,

$$\frac{3\times[CS(\bar{y},x\ )]^2}{CS(x\ ,x)} = \frac{3\times 75.0649}{10} = 22.51947\ .$$

The sum of squares due to times $= 3\times(3.368^2 + \ldots + 0.245^2) - C.F.$
$= 22.692.$

Out total sum of squares, adjusted for the general mean, is

$$(3.401^2 + 2.186^2 + \ldots + 0.000^2) - \text{correction} = 22.9512.$$

The analysis of variance table is therefore:

Source	CSS	df	MS
Regression	22.5195	1	22.5195
Deviations	0.1725	3	0.0575
Due to time	22.6920	4	5.6730
Residual	0.2592	10	0.0259
Total	22.9512	14	

1. cont'd.

To test the significance of the regression, we find $F = \frac{22.5195}{0.0259} = 869.40$

The 0.1% level of $F(1,10)$ is 21.0.

2. Our first regression model is $\bar{y}_i = \bar{y}. + \beta(x_i - \bar{x}) + \varepsilon_{ij}$.

The regression sum of squares $= \frac{2 \times [CS(\bar{y}, x)]^2}{CS(x, x)}$

$$= \frac{2 \times (42868.1475)^2}{815037.75} = 4509.43 .$$

The total corrected sum of squares $= 3.61^2 + \ldots + 38.66^2 - 32 \times \bar{y}^2 = 5066.597$.

The sum of squares due to time of sampling $= 3.58^2 + \ldots + 37.70^2 - 32 \times \bar{y}^2$

$$= 4971.412.$$

Analysis of Variance Table

Source	CSS	df	MS
Regression	4509.430	1	4509.430
Deviations	461.982	14	32.999
Due to time	4971.412	15	331.427
Residuals	95.185	16	5.949
Total	5066.597	31	

The F value for the regression of $\frac{4509.43}{5.949} = 758.0$ is highly significant

However, the deviations F value of $\frac{32.999}{5.949} = 5.547$ is also significant,

so we need another model. Since we cannot use orthogonal polynomials, any model involving higher order terms is messy. Moreover, a graph showing % age weight loss plotted against date of sampling suggests a square root transformation. Our model is then

$$\bar{y}_i = \bar{y}. + \beta(x_i^* - \bar{x}^*) + \varepsilon_{ij}$$

where x^* represents the transformed time values.

The regression sum of squares $= \frac{2 \times [CS(\bar{y}_i, x_i^*)]^2}{CS(x_i^*, x_i^*)}$

$$= \frac{2 \times [7290.39303 - 5891.93042]^2}{5122 - 4298.67218}$$

$$= 4750.71441$$

2. cont'd.

Analysis of Variance Table

Source	CSS	df	MS
Regression	4750.714	1	4750.714
Deviations	220.698	14	15.764
Due to time of sampling	4971.412	15	331.427
Residuals	95.185	16	5.949
Total	5066.597	31	

This time the deviations F value is $\frac{15.764}{5.949} = 2.65$, which is barely significant at the 5% level.

If an analysis is carried through on the untransformed variable x, the addition of higher order terms is straightforward using a computer. However, the addition of higher order terms in such models often produces very high correlations with existing terms in the model, and sometimes problems occur in the numerical methods due to this.

3. The model is

$$y_{ij} = \mu + \beta_1 f_1(x_i) + \beta_2 f_2(x_i) + \beta_3 f_3(x_i) + \beta_4 f_4(x_i) + \epsilon_{ij}$$

where $i = 1,2,\ldots,k$, and $j = 1,2,\ldots,n$. Since the polynomials are orthogonal we have

$$\sum_i f_r(x_i) = 0$$

$$\sum_{r \neq s}\sum f_r(x_i) f_s(x_i) = 0.$$

On writing out the matrix $\underline{a}$ we quickly get

$$\underline{a}'\underline{a} = \begin{pmatrix} kn & & & 0 \\ & n\sum_i f_1^2(x_i) & & \\ & & \ddots & \\ 0 & & & n\sum_i f_4^2(x_i) \end{pmatrix}$$

From this form of the design matrix we now see that

$$S_{reg} = kn(\hat{\mu})^2 + n\hat{\beta}_1^2 \sum_i f_1^2(x_i) + \ldots + n\hat{\beta}_4^2 \sum_i f_4^2(x_i) .$$

4. Our basic model is $y_{ij} = \bar{y}_{i.} + \varepsilon_{ij}$. The within-groups variance $= \sum\limits_{ij}\sum \varepsilon_{ij}^2 = \sum\limits_{ij}\sum (y_{ij} - \bar{y}_{i.})^2$. The between groups variance is equal to Total CSS - within-groups CSS

$$= \sum_{ij}\sum (y_{ij} - \bar{y}_{..})^2 - \sum_{ij}\sum (y_{ij} - \bar{y}_{i.})^2$$
$$= \sum_{ij}\sum \bar{y}_{..}^2 + \sum_{ij}\sum y_{ij}\bar{y}_{i.} - 2\sum_{ij}\sum y_{ij}\bar{y}_{..}$$
$$= \sum_i n_i(\bar{y}_{i.} - \bar{y}_{..})^2 \ .$$

The $S_{reg} = \dfrac{[CS(x,y)]^2}{CS(x,x)}$

$$CS(x,y) = \sum_{ij}\sum (y_{ij} - \bar{y}_{..})(x_i - \bar{x}) = \sum_i n_i(\bar{y}_{i.} - \bar{y}_{..})(x_i - \bar{x})$$
$$CS(x,x) = \sum_i n_i(x_i - \bar{x})^2$$
$$\therefore S_{reg} = \frac{[\sum_i n_i(\bar{y}_{i.} - \bar{y}_{..})(x_i - \bar{x})]^2}{\sum_i n_i(x_i - \bar{x})^2}$$

EXERCISES 11.2

1. From chapter 5, $\hat{\underline{\theta}} = (\underline{a}'\underline{a})^{-1}\underline{a}'\underline{Y}$ and $V(\hat{\underline{\theta}}) = (\underline{a}'\underline{a})^{-1}\hat{\sigma}^2$

$$\therefore \hat{\beta} = \frac{1}{140}(-5 \times 7.7 \quad -3 \times 7.9 \ \ldots + 5 \times 3.6) = -\frac{23}{140} = -0.164$$
$$V(\hat{\beta}) = \frac{1}{140}\hat{\sigma}^2 = .00038.$$

EXERCISES 11.3

1.a) Using linear contrasts, we have the following

Days totals	550	527	526	545	$\frac{(\sum_i f_i T_i)}{5\sum f_i^2}$
Linear	-3	-1	1	3	2.56
Quadratic	1	-1	-1	1	88.20
Cubic	-1	3	-3	1	.04
					90.80

90.80 is, of course, the between days CSS.

b) We are considering a response surface. To subdivide the Days × Pressures Linear sum of squares, we have to weight the linear contrasts already formed, (see Table 11.15).

	-22	-32	-55	-38	A	B	SS
$D_L \times P_L$	-3	-1	1	3	-71	200	25.205
$D_Q \times P_L$	1	-1	-1	1	27	40	18.225
$D_C \times P_L$	-1	3	-3	1	53	200	14.045
							57.475

1.b) cont'd.

These calculations are carried out as follows:

$$(-3)(-22) + (-1)(-32) + (1)(-55) + (3)(-38) = -71$$

$$((-3)^2 + (-1)^2 + (1)^2 + (3)^2) \Sigma f_j^2 = 200$$

where the (f_j) represent the values of the linear polynomials used earlier.

C H A P T E R   T W E L V E

An Analysis of Data on Trees

EXERCISES 12.4

1. The two models are

$$y_{ij} = \alpha_i + \beta_{1i}(w_{ij} - \bar{w}_{i.}) + \beta_{2i}(x_{ij} - \bar{x}_{i.}) + \varepsilon_{ij}$$

and

$$y_{ij} = \alpha + \beta_1(w_{ij} - \bar{w}_{i.}) + \beta_2(x_{ij} - \bar{x}_{i.}) + \varepsilon_{ij}.$$

The difference in CSS of 0.010751 is produced by allowing for rootstock differences in means and regression coefficients. Since a further 9 degrees of freedom are needed for this, the resulting MS is 0.001195, which is not very different from the estimated error variance of 0.001225. Essentially, it is the difference due to fitting one or four regression lines.

3. The recommended equation is

$$y_{ij} = 2.149 + 1.43(w_{ij} - \bar{w}_{i.}) + 0.638(x_{ij} - \bar{x}_{i.}) + \varepsilon_{ij}\ .$$

4. Model 1: $y_{ij} = \alpha_i + \beta_{1i}(w_{ij} - \bar{w}_{i.}) + \beta_{2i}(x_{ij} - \bar{x}_{i.}) + \varepsilon_{ij}$.
cf. equation 1 in section 11.2.

$S_{par} = 0.178856$
$S_{min} = 0.029399.$

Model 2: $y_{ij} = \alpha_i + \beta_1(w_{ij} - \bar{w}_{i.}) + \beta_2(x_{ij} - \bar{x}_{i.}) + \varepsilon_{ij}$.
cf. equation 2 in section 11.2.

$S_{par} = 1.013492$
$S_{min} = 0.036973$

Model 3: $y_{ij} = \alpha_i + \beta_1(w_{ij} - \bar{w}_{i.}) + \beta_{2i}(x_{ij} - \bar{x}_{i.}) + \varepsilon_{ij}$.

$S_{par} = 1.019394$
$S_{min} = 0.031071$.

4. cont'd.

Model 4: $y_{ij} = \alpha_t + \beta_{1i}(w_{ij} - \bar{w}_{i.}) + \beta_2(x_{ij} - \bar{x}_{i.}) + \varepsilon_{ij}$.

$S_{par} = 1.019226$

$S_{min} = 0.031239$.

Models 3 and 4 are extensions of model 2.

Model 5: $y_{ij} = \alpha + \beta_1(w_{ij} - \bar{w}_{i.}) + \beta_2(x_{ij} - \bar{x}_{i.}) + \varepsilon_{ij}$.

cf. equation 3 in section 11.2

$S_{par} = 1.010315$

$S_{min} = 0.040150$.

5. H_o is that in model 2, all the regression SS are due to the α_i

	CSS	df	MS
Regression using model 2	1.013492	5	0.202698
Regression on α_i alone	0.842209	3	
Due to β's	0.171283	2	0.085642 .

Our estimate of σ^2 for model 2 is 0.001232. Then

$$F = \frac{0.085642}{0.001232} = 69.5146 \quad \text{on (2.30) df.}$$

Therefore we reject this hypothesis.

CHAPTER THIRTEEN

The Analysis of Variance: Subsidiary Analyses

EXERCISES 13.2

1. See the reference given for an answer to a similar problem.

2. A reduction in degrees of freedom for error marginally favours the *T*-method of comparison. For example, if we assume one degree of freedom for error then the entry for the (2,4) contrast in the table of Scheffé, 1959, p.77, changes from 0.51 to 0.53.

Exercises 13.7

1. The Box-Cox method on Ex.13.4 results in a value of λ in the transformation (8.5) of about 0.5. The actual maximum of the likelihood is nearer 0.4, and approximate 95% confidence intervals for λ are 0.01 to 0.69. This therefore leads to the same transformation as was used in the text.

2. Due to the nature of the experiment it is advisable to take logarithms in order to create an additive model (see also Wooding(1969)).

Table of (natural) log transforms of the original data

Treatment		*A*	*B*	*C*	*D*	Mean
Animal	1	0.0000	0.2231	0.4055	0.6932	0.3305
	2	0.4055	0.5596	0.9163	1.2528	0.7836
	3	0.9163	1.0986	1.3863	1.2528	1.1635
	4	1.0986	0.6932	1.0986	0.9163	0.9517
	5	0.4055	0.6932	0.9163	1.2528	0.8170
	6	0.4055	0.2231	0.6932	1.0986	0.6051
	7	0.4055	0.6932	0.9163	0.9163	0.7328
	8	0.6932	0.6932	0.9163	1.3863	0.9223
Mean		0.5413	0.6097	0.9061	1.0961	0.7883

The calculations for the analysis of variance are as follows.

Sum of Squares	Total	Treatment	Animal
U.S.S.	23.8556	21.4974	21.6148
Correction	19.8847	19.8847	19.8847
C.S.S.	3.9709	1.6127	1.7301

This leads to the following 'ANOVA' table.

Source	S.S.	d.f.	M.S.	F
Animals	1.7301	7	0.2472	8.27
Treatments	1.6127	3	0.5376	17.98
Error	0.6281	21	0.0299	
Total	3.9709	31		

The 0.1% value on (3,21) degrees of freedom in the F-tables is 7.94 so we have very good evidence of a difference in the treatment means.

The factor for the T-method at the 5% level of significance for comparing the difference of two treatment means is

$$3.95 \times \sqrt{0.0299/8} = 0.24$$

so the treatment can be divided into pairs

(A,B), (C,D)

such that there are differences between pairs but not within pairs. The 0.1% value on (7,21) degrees of freedom in the F-tables is 5.56 and so we note that the use of blocking has been effective.

The analysis of residuals is left to the reader although it is noted here that animal 4 appears to be an outlier since it does not exhibit the pattern shown by the remaining animals and this should be investigated.

C H A P T E R   F O U R T E E N

Random Effects Models

EXERCISES 14.2

1. A 99% confidence interval for λ for Ex.14.1 data is as follows:-

$$C.I. = \frac{1}{r}\left\{\frac{S_b^2}{S_w^2\, F_{1-\frac{\alpha}{2}}(\nu_b,\nu_w)} - 1\right\},\ \frac{1}{r}\left\{\frac{S_b^2}{S_w^2\, F_{\frac{\alpha}{2}}(\nu_b,\nu_w)} - 1\right\}$$

$$= \tfrac{1}{4}\left\{\frac{4.646}{1.409\times F_{.995}(5,18)} - 1\right\},\ \tfrac{1}{4}\left\{\frac{4.646}{1.409\times F_{.005}(18,5)} - 1\right\}$$

$$= \tfrac{1}{4}\left\{\frac{4.646}{1.409\times 4.96} - 1\right\},\quad \tfrac{1}{4}\left\{\frac{4.646\ \ 13.0}{1.409} - 1\right\}$$

$$= (-\ .084,\ \ 10.466)\ .$$

Write this as (0,10.466) with the lower limit truncated at 0.

2. A 95% confidence interval for is as follows:-

$$\frac{\nu_b s_b^2}{\sigma^2+r\sigma_\alpha^2} \sim \chi^2_{\nu_b} \quad \text{and} \quad \frac{\nu_w s_w^2}{\sigma^2} \sim \chi^2_{\nu_w}$$

$$F = s_b^2/s_w^2 = 3.3$$
$$\alpha = .05$$
$$F_1 = F_{.975}(5,18) = 3.38$$
$$F_2 = F_{.975}(5,\infty) = 2.56$$
$$F_3 = F_{.975}(18,5) = 6.40$$
$$F_4 = F_{.975}(\infty,5) = 6.02$$

$$C.I. = \{(F-F_1)(F+F_1-F_2)/FF_2\}\frac{S_w^2}{r},\ \left\{FF_4 - 1 + \frac{(F_3-F_4)}{FF_3^2}\right\}\frac{S_w^2}{r}$$

$$= \{(3.3-3.38)(3.3+3.38-1.79)/3.3\times 2.56\}\frac{1.409}{4}$$

$$\{(3.3\times 6.53) - 1 + \frac{6.4-6.53}{3.3\times 6.4^2}\}\frac{1.409}{4},$$

$$+\ (-.014, 7.238).$$

Write this as (0,7.238), with the lower limit truncated at 0.

3. We have $\hat{\lambda} = \hat{\sigma}_\alpha^2/\hat{\sigma}^2$, and

$$V(\hat{\sigma}_\alpha^2/\hat{\sigma}^2) = \left(\frac{d\hat{\lambda}}{d\hat{\sigma}_\alpha^2}\right)^2 V(\hat{\sigma}_\alpha^2) + \left(\frac{d\hat{\lambda}}{d\hat{\sigma}^2}\right) V(\hat{\sigma}^2) .$$

This leads to the following:

$$V(\hat{\lambda}) = \frac{1}{\sigma^4}\ \frac{2}{r^2}\left(\frac{(\sigma^2+r\sigma_\alpha^2)}{\nu_b} + \frac{\sigma^4}{\nu_w}\right) + \frac{2\sigma_\alpha^4}{\sigma^2\nu_w}$$

$$= \frac{1}{\sigma^4}\ \frac{2}{r^2}\left(\frac{(\sigma^2 + r\sigma_\alpha^2)^2}{\nu_b} + \frac{\sigma^4}{\nu_w} + \frac{r^2\sigma_\alpha^4}{\nu_w}\right)$$

$$= \frac{1}{\sigma^4}\ \frac{2}{r^2}\left(\frac{\sigma^4 + 2r\sigma^2\sigma_\alpha^2+r^2\sigma_\alpha^4}{\nu_b} + \frac{\sigma^2 + r^2\sigma_\alpha^4}{\nu_w}\right)$$

$$= \frac{2}{r^2}\left(\frac{1+2r\lambda+r^2\lambda^2}{\nu_b} + \frac{1+r^2\lambda^2}{\nu_w}\right)$$

$$= \frac{2}{r^2\nu_b} + \frac{4r\lambda}{r^2\nu} + \frac{2\ {}^2\lambda^2}{r^2\nu_b} + \frac{2}{r^2\nu_w} + \frac{2r^2\lambda^2}{r^2\nu_w}$$

$$= \frac{2}{r^2\nu_b} + \frac{4\lambda}{r\nu_b} + \frac{2\lambda^2}{\nu_b} + \frac{2}{{}^2\nu_w} + \frac{2\lambda^2}{\nu_w}$$

$$= 2\left(\lambda^2 + \frac{2\lambda}{r} + \frac{1}{r^2}\right)\left(\frac{1}{\nu_b} + \frac{1}{\nu_w}\right) - \frac{4\lambda}{r\nu_w}$$

$$= \left(\lambda + \frac{1}{r}\right)^2\left(\frac{2}{\nu_b} + \frac{2}{\nu_w}\right) - \frac{4}{r\nu_w}$$

$$\approx \left(\lambda + \frac{1}{r}\right)^2\left(\frac{2}{\nu_b} + \frac{2}{\nu_w}\right) .$$

4. We proceed as follows:

$$V = \frac{\sigma^2 + r\sigma_\alpha^2}{rt}$$

$$C = \gamma t + rt \Rightarrow t = c/(\alpha+r) .$$

Therefore

$$V = (\sigma^2 + r\sigma_\alpha^2)(\gamma + r)/rC$$

$$= \frac{\sigma^2\gamma}{rc} + \frac{\sigma^2}{c} + \frac{\gamma\sigma_\alpha^2}{c} + \frac{r\sigma_\alpha^2}{c}$$

$$\frac{dV}{dr} = \frac{\sigma_\alpha^2}{c} - \frac{\sigma^2\gamma}{cr^2} = 0 .$$

4. cont'd.
Therefore

$$\frac{\sigma^2_\alpha}{\sigma^2} = \frac{\gamma}{r^2} \quad \text{so} \quad r = \sqrt{\gamma/\lambda}$$

and so $t = c/(\gamma+r)$

$$= c/(\gamma+\sqrt{\gamma/\lambda})$$

$$= c\sqrt{\lambda}/(\gamma\sqrt{\lambda} + \sqrt{\gamma})$$

$$t = c\sqrt{\lambda}/\sqrt{\gamma}(\sqrt{\lambda\gamma}+1) \; .$$

Hence the result (14.14).

5. Variances of t and r.

$$V(f(Y_1,Y_2)) = \left(\frac{df}{dY_1}\right)^2 V(Y_1) + \left(\frac{df}{dY_2}\right)^2 V(Y_2)$$

$$r = \frac{\sqrt{\gamma}}{\sqrt{\lambda}}, \quad V(r) = \left(\frac{dr}{d\sqrt{\gamma}}\right)^2 V(\sqrt{\gamma}) + \left(\frac{dr}{d\hat{\lambda}}\right)^2 V(\hat{\lambda})$$

$$= 0 + [-\tfrac{1}{2}\sqrt{\gamma}\,\hat{\lambda}^{-3/2}]^2 V(\hat{\lambda})$$

$$\therefore \; V(r) = \frac{\gamma}{4\lambda^3}\left(\lambda + \frac{1}{r}\right)^2 \left(\frac{2}{\nu_b} + \frac{2}{\nu_w}\right)$$

$$t = \frac{c\sqrt{\lambda}}{\sqrt{\gamma} + \gamma\sqrt{\lambda}} = \frac{c}{r+\gamma}$$

$$V(t) = \left(\frac{dt}{dc}\right)^2 V(c) + \left(\frac{dt}{dr}\right)^2 V(r)$$

$$= 0 + -c(r+\gamma)^{-2} V(r)$$

$$\therefore \; V(t) = \frac{c}{(r+\gamma)^4\, 4\lambda^3}\left(\lambda + \frac{1}{r}\right)^2 \left(\frac{2}{\nu_b} + \frac{2}{\nu_w}\right) .$$

6. The analysis of variance is as follows:-

Source of variation	S.S.	d.f.	M.S.	E(MS)
Between machines	212.595	11	19.327	$\sigma^2 + 4\sigma^2_\alpha$
Within machines	157.805	36	4.383	σ^2
Total	370.4	47		

As F is 4.41 on (11,36), we reject the hypothesis that $\sigma^2_\alpha = 0$.

Components of variance

$\hat{\sigma}^2_\alpha$ = Within machine MS = 4.383;

$\hat{\sigma}^2_\alpha$ = (Between machines-Within machines MS)/4 = 3.736.

The variation between lengths (within each machine) accounts for over 50% of variation in data.

If three different weeks were used, a sum of squares between weeks would have to be calculated.

7(*a*) The following results are obtained:

Source of Variation	S.S.	d.f.	M.S.
Between films	24.08	7	3.44
Within films	9.31	16	0.582
Total	33.39	23	

$\hat{\sigma}^2 = .582$

$\hat{\sigma}^2_\alpha = (3.44 - .582)/3 = .953$.

$$90\%\ C.I.\ \text{ for } \lambda : \frac{1}{3}\left\{\frac{3.44}{.582\ F_{.95}(7,16)} - 1\right\},\ \frac{1}{3}\left\{\frac{3.44}{.582\ F_{.05}(16,7)} - 1\right\}$$

$$= \frac{1}{3}\left\{\frac{3.44}{.582,\ 2.66} - 1\right\},\ \frac{1}{3}\left\{\frac{3.44,\ 3.517}{.582} - 1\right\}$$

$$= (.4073,\ 6.596).$$

(*b*) $\gamma = 7, \quad \hat{\lambda} = 1.637$

$r = \sqrt{\gamma/\hat{\lambda}} = \sqrt{7/1.637} = \sqrt{4.27} = 2.066.$

Therefore 2 measurements should be made on each film.

(*c*) To minimise $V(\bar{X})$, $r = 2.066$, $t = C\sqrt{\lambda}/(\sqrt{\gamma}(\sqrt{\lambda\gamma}+1))$

C (Expenditure), from above is

$t + rt = 80$

$t = 80 \times 1.279/(2.646(4385))$

$= 82.$

Therefore 9 films should be used, and 2 observations on each should be taken, in order to minimise $V(\bar{X})$ for an expenditure of C.

EXERCISES 14.3

1. Point estimates of $\sigma^2, \sigma^2_\alpha, \sigma^2_\beta$.

Using notation of p.289,

$E(C) = \sigma^2 = E(\hat{\sigma}^2) \Rightarrow \hat{\sigma}^2 = C$

$E(B) = \sigma^2 + r\sigma^2_\beta$.

Therefore

$$\sigma^2_\beta = \frac{E(B) = E(C)}{r} = E(\hat{\sigma}^2_\beta) \Rightarrow \hat{\sigma}^2_\beta = (B-C)/r$$

$$E(A) = \sigma^2 + r\sigma^2_\beta + rq\sigma^2_\alpha$$

$$= E(B) + rq\sigma^2_\alpha$$

$$\sigma^2_\alpha = \frac{E(A) - E(B)}{rq} = E(\hat{\sigma}^2_\alpha) \Rightarrow \hat{\sigma}^2_\alpha = (A-B)/rq\ .$$

1. cont'd.

Variances

$$V(\hat{\sigma}^2) = V(C)$$

$$pq\,\frac{(r-1)}{\sigma^2} \sim \chi^2_{pq(r-1)} \;.$$

Therefore

$$V(C) = V(\hat{\sigma}^2) = \frac{2\sigma^4}{pq(r-1)}$$

so

$$\text{est.}V(\sigma^2) = \frac{2C^2}{pq(r-1)}$$

$$\frac{p(q-1)B}{\sigma^2+r\sigma^2_\beta} \sim \chi^2_{p(q-1)} \;.$$

Therefore

$$V(B) = \frac{2(\sigma^2+r\sigma^2_\beta)}{p(q-1)} \;.$$

Therefore

$$V(\sigma^2_\beta) = \frac{1}{r^2}\,(V(B) + V(C))$$

$$= \frac{2}{r^2}\left(\frac{(\sigma^2+r\sigma^2_\beta)^2}{p(q-1)} + \frac{\sigma^4}{pq(r-1)}\right)$$

and

$$\text{est.}V(\hat{\sigma}^2_\beta) = \frac{2}{r^2}\left(\frac{B^2}{p(q-1)} + \frac{C^2}{pq(r-1)}\right) \;.$$

Finally,

$$\frac{(p-1)A}{(\sigma^2+r\sigma^2_\beta+rq\sigma^2_\alpha)} \sim \chi^2_{(p-1)} \;.$$

Therefore

$$V(A) = 2(\sigma^2+r\sigma^2_\beta+rq\sigma^2_\alpha)^2/(p-1)$$

$$V(\hat{\sigma}^2_\alpha) = \frac{1}{r^2q^2}\,(V(A) + V(B))$$

$$= \frac{1}{r^2q^2}\left(\frac{2(\sigma^2+r\sigma^2_\beta+rq\sigma^2_\alpha)^2}{p-1} + \frac{2(\sigma^2+r\sigma^2_\beta)^2}{p(q-1)}\right)$$

and

$$\text{est.}V(\hat{\sigma}^2_\alpha) = \frac{2}{r^2q^2}\;\frac{A^2}{p-1} + \frac{B^2}{p(q-1)} \;.$$

EXERCISES 14.4

1. Anova table:

Source	C.S.S.	d.f.	M.S.	E(MS)
Between times	.1153	6	.0192	$\sigma^2+2\sigma^2_\beta+6\sigma^2_\alpha$
Between samples within times	.4047	14	.0289	$\sigma^2+2\sigma^2_\beta$
Between determinations within samples	.1650	21	.0079	σ^2
Total	.6850	41		

1. cont'd.

Components of variance:

$\hat{\sigma}^2 = .0079$

$\hat{\sigma}^2_\beta = .0105$

$\hat{\sigma}^2_\alpha = -,0016$.

To test for $\sigma^2_\alpha = 0$, $F = \dfrac{.0289}{.0079} = 3.66$, and from the tables

$F(6,14) > .664$ for 5%

so it seems as though $\sigma^2_\alpha = 0$.

We see that the largest component of variance is that for between samples.

2. Anova table:

Source	C.S.S.	d.f.	M.S.	E(MS)
Between lots	133.72	12	11.14	$\sigma^2+2\sigma^2_\alpha+4\sigma^2_\beta+8\sigma^2_\alpha$
Between samples within lots	3.006	13	.231	$\sigma^2+2\sigma^2_\alpha+4\sigma^2_\beta$
Between chemists within samples	3.428	26	.132	$\sigma^2+2\sigma^2_\sigma$
Between determinations	2.546	52	.049	σ^2
Total	142.7	103		

Components of variance

$\hat{\sigma}^2 = .049$

$\hat{\sigma}^2_\alpha = .0415$

$\sigma^2_\beta = .025$

$\sigma^2_\alpha = 1.364$

σ^2_α: $F = 11.14/.231 = 48.23$, and $F(12,13) \ll 48.23$,

so there is strong evidence to suggest $\sigma^2_\alpha \neq 0$.

σ^2_β: $F = .231/.132 = 1.75$, and $F(13,26) > 1.75$,

giving some evidence to suggest $\sigma^2_\beta > 0$.

σ^2_α: $F = .132/.049 = 2.69$, and $F(26,52) < 2.69$,

suggesting $\sigma^2_\alpha = 0$.

Thus most of the variation in the data arises from between lots.

EXERCISES 14.5

1.

M.S.	d.f.	E(MS)
A	V_A	$\sigma^2 + r(1-q/Q)\tau_\beta^2 + rq\tau_\alpha^2$
B	V_B	$\sigma^2 + r\tau_\beta^2$
C	V_C	σ^2

$$\frac{\nu_C C}{\sigma^2} \sim \chi^2_{\nu_C} \quad \text{therefore} \quad V(C) = \frac{2\sigma^4}{\nu_C}$$

$$\frac{\nu_B B}{\sigma^2 + r\tau_\beta^2} \sim \chi^2_{\nu_B} \text{ therefore} \quad V(B) = \frac{2(\sigma^2 + r\tau_\beta^2)^2}{\nu_B}$$

$$\frac{\nu_A A}{\sigma^2 + r(1-q/Q)\tau_\beta^2 + rq\tau_\alpha^2} \sim \chi^2_{\nu_A} \text{ therefore } V(A) = 2(\sigma^2 + r(1-q/Q)\tau_\beta^2 + rq\tau_\alpha^2)^2/V_C$$

Now, $\tau_\alpha^2 = \{MS(A) - (1-q/Q)MS(B) - (q/Q)MS(C)\}/rq$.

$$\text{Therefore} \quad V(\tau_\alpha^2) = \frac{1}{r^2q^2}\{V(A) - (1-q/Q)^2V(B) + q^2/Q^2\, V(C)\}$$

$$= \frac{2}{r^2q^2}\left\{\frac{(\sigma^2 + r(1-q/Q)\tau_\beta^2 + rq\tau_\alpha^2)}{\nu_A} + \frac{(1-q/Q)^2(\sigma^2 + r\tau_\beta^2)}{\nu_B} + \frac{\sigma^4}{\nu_C}\right\}.$$

2. $E(B) = \sigma^2 + r\tau_\beta^2$.

Therefore

$$\tau_\beta^2 = \frac{E(B) - E(A)}{r}$$

$$\hat{\tau}_\beta^2 = \frac{B - A}{r} \quad .$$

$$\text{Therefore} \quad V(\hat{\tau}_\beta^2) = \frac{1}{r^2}(V(B) + V(A))$$

$$= \frac{1}{r^2}\left(\frac{2(\sigma^2 + r\tau_\beta^2)^2}{\nu_B} + \frac{2(\sigma^2 + r(1-q/Q)\tau_\beta^2 + rq\tau_\alpha^2}{\nu_A}\right) .$$

EXERCISES 14.7

1. To show independence among the sums of squares we need to show that $(\bar{y}_{i..} - \bar{y}_{...})$, $(\bar{y}_{ij.} - \bar{y}_{i..})$ and $(y_{ijk} - \bar{y}_{ij.})$ are uncorrelated.

We can write

$$(\bar{y}_{i..} - \bar{y}_{...}) = \hat{\alpha}_i$$
$$(y_{ij.} - \bar{y}_{i..}) = \hat{\beta}_{j(i)}$$
$$(y_{ijk} - \bar{y}_{ij.}) = \varepsilon_{ijk}.$$

From the theory of chapter 10, for example, we can find the variance-covariance matrix of the estimated parameters, and establish that the relevant covariances are zero.

2. See the discussion in Davies (1967).

3. See chapter 8 of 'Fitting equations to data' by C.Daniel and F.S.Wood, John Wiley,(1971).

CHAPTER FIFTEEN

Crossed Classifications

EXERCISES 15.3

1. The algebra is straightforward, if tedious. For example,

$$y_{ijk} = \mu + \phi_{ij} + \varepsilon_{ijk}$$

$$\bar{y}_{ij.} = \mu + \phi_{ij} + \bar{\varepsilon}_{ij.} \quad .$$

$$\therefore \; E\left[\frac{\sum\sum\sum_{ijk}(y_{ijk} - \bar{y}_{ij.})^2}{rc(n-1)}\right] = \frac{1}{rc(n-1)}\sum\sum\sum_{ijk} E(\varepsilon_{ijk} - \bar{\varepsilon}_{ij.})^2 \; .$$

By an elementary result

$$\frac{1}{(n-1)} E\sum_k(\varepsilon_{ijk} - \bar{\varepsilon}_{ij.})^2 = \sigma^2 \; .$$

Hence $E(\text{Mean square } B) = \sigma^2$.

2. See Scheffé's Analysis of Variance, Wiley (1959), p.126, for discussion of this point.

EXERCISES 15.4

1.

$$\bar{y}_{ij.} = \mu + \alpha_i + \beta_j + \bar{\varepsilon}_{ij.}$$

$$\bar{y}_{i..} = \mu + \alpha_i + \bar{\beta}_. + \bar{\varepsilon}_{i..}$$

$$\bar{y}_{.j.} = \mu + \bar{\alpha}_. + \beta_j + \bar{\varepsilon}_{.j.}$$

$$\bar{y}_{...} = \mu + \bar{\alpha}_. + \bar{\beta}_. + \bar{\varepsilon}_{...} \; .$$

Then $r_{ij} = \bar{\varepsilon}_{ij.} - \bar{\varepsilon}_{i..} - \bar{\varepsilon}_{.j.} + \bar{\varepsilon}_{...}$.

$$\begin{aligned} V(r_{ij}) = {} & V(\bar{\varepsilon}_{ij.}) + V(\bar{\varepsilon}_{i..}) + V(\bar{\varepsilon}_{.j.}) + V(\bar{\varepsilon}_{...}) \\ & - 2C(\bar{\varepsilon}_{ij.},\bar{\varepsilon}_{i..}) - 2C(\bar{\varepsilon}_{ij.},\bar{\varepsilon}_{.j.}) + 2C(\bar{\varepsilon}_{ij.},\bar{\varepsilon}_{...}) \\ & + 2C(\bar{\varepsilon}_{i..},\bar{\varepsilon}_{.j.}) - 2C(\bar{\varepsilon}_{i..},\bar{\varepsilon}_{...}) - 2C(\bar{\varepsilon}_{.j.},\bar{\varepsilon}_{...}) \end{aligned}$$

1. cont'd.

$$= \sigma^2\left(\frac{1}{n} + \frac{1}{cn} + \frac{1}{rn} + \frac{1}{ncr} - \frac{2}{cn} - \frac{2}{rn} + \frac{2}{ncr} + \frac{2}{ncr} - \frac{2}{ncr} - \frac{2}{ncr}\right)$$

$$= \sigma^2 \frac{(r-1)(c-1)}{rcn} .$$

$C(r_{ij}\ r_{hk}) = E(r_{ij.}\ r_{hk})$ since $E(r_{ij}) = 0$. Using the same method as in the first part, we find that most of the terms equal zero, and the rest sum to σ^2/rcn .

3. Analysis of Variance Table

Source	CSS	df	MS
Reagent	120	3	40
Catalyst	48	2	24
Interaction	84	6	14
Between	252	11	
Within	48	12	4
Total	300	23	

The interaction mean square is significant.

A graph of the results shows a strong interaction component. It is best simply to state which combinations of reagent and catalyst give the best results.

C H A P T E R   S I X T E E N

Further Analysis of Variance

EXERCISES 16.1

1. The numbers of degrees of freedom can be justified by arguments similar to those used in §15.3 and §10.4.

EXERCISES 16.2

1. This is a three-way crossed classification experiment and from the data we get the following ANOVA table.

Source	C.S.S.	d.f.	M.S.	F
SSA	41027.17	2	20513.6	203.99
SSB	220.03	1	220.03	2.19
SSC	8278.92	5	1655.78	16.47
SSAB	533.38	2	266.69	2.65
SSAC	391.16	5	78.23	.78
SSBC	1064.47	10	106.45	1.06
Residual	1005.62	10	100.56	
Total	52520.75	35		

The tabulated 5% value for the required F-distributions are:-

$$F(2.10) = 4.10$$
$$F(1,10) = 4.96$$
$$F(5,10) = 3.33$$
$$F(10,10) = 2.98 .$$

From the Anova table, it appears that the B factor main effect is insignificant, as are the interaction effects. The variability in the data seems to be due to factors A and C, particularly A .

2. Treating each setting station in turn, we form 4 two-way analyses of variance.

A

Source	d.f.	C.S.S.	M.S.	F
Testing stations	3	0.2	.067	2.094
Regulators	7	2.745	.392	
Error	21	0.67	.032	
Total	31	3.615		

B

Source	d.f.	C.S.S.	M.S.	F
Testing stations	3	.5225	.174	2.0
Regulators	3	.3125	.104	1.197
Error	9	.7825	.087	
Total	15	1.6175		

C

Source	d.f.	C.S.S.	M.S.	F
Testing stations	3	.0843	.0281	.774
Regulators	6	.8725	.1454	4.01
Error	18	.6528	.0363	
Total	27	1.6096		

D

Source	d.f.	C.S.S.	M.S.	F
Testing stations	3	0.06	0.02	0.167
Regulators	6	0.72	0.12	5.71
Error	18	.384	.021	
Total	27	1.164		

In all cases the mean squares for regulators are significant at the 5% level.

A combined analysis is as follows:-

Source	C.S.S.	d.f.	M.S.	F	
Setting stations	2.33	3	.78	19.5	*
Testing stations	.56	3	.19	4.75	*
Setting × testing	.3	9	.03	0.75	
Regulators within setting stations	4.65	22	.21	5.25	*
Error	2.49	66	.04		
Total	10.33	103			

* significant at the 5% level.

From this point it is possible to estimate components of variance between and within setting stations. See the original reference for a discussion of the data and analysis.

CHAPTER SEVENTEEN

The generalised linear model

EXERCISES 17.3

1. Firstly

$$E\left(\frac{\partial^2 L}{\partial \mu^2}\right) = E\{Y\,a''(\mu) - b''(\mu)\}/\phi$$
$$= \{\mu\,a''(\mu) - b''(\mu)\}/\ \phi$$

using (17.12), and also

$$E\left(\frac{\partial L}{\partial \mu}\right)^2 = E\{(Y\,a'(\mu) - b'(\mu))/\phi\}^2$$
$$= E\{Y^2\ a'(\mu)^2 + b'(\mu)^2 - Y\ a'(\mu)b'(y)\}/\phi^2$$
$$= E(Y^2)\ a'(\mu)^2/\phi^2,$$

once again using (17.12).
Hence from (17.13) we have

$$E(Y^2) = \left(\frac{\phi}{a'(\mu)}\right)^2 \{b''(\mu) - \mu\ a''(\mu)\}$$

and so

$$V(Y) = E(Y^2) - E(Y)^2$$
$$= \left(\frac{\phi}{a'(\mu)}\right)^2 \{b''(\mu) - \mu a''(\mu)\} - \left(\frac{b'(\mu)}{a'(\mu)}\right)^2 .$$

EXERCISES 17.6

1. Since the distributions of all counts are assumed to be Poisson, we have case (2) of table 17.1. If we assume independence of the variables then the model to be fitted is

$$E(Y_{ij}) = \mu_{ij} \simeq \mu_{i.}\,\mu_{.j}/\mu_{..}\,.$$

where $\mu_{..}$ is the overall mean effect, $\mu_{i.}$ is the effect of category i of variable 1 and $\mu_{.j}$ is the effect of category j of variable 2. Thus the link function is

$$\eta_{ij} = \log \mu_{ij} = -\log \mu_{..} + \log \mu_{i.} + \log \mu_{ij}$$
$$= \mu + \alpha_i + \beta_j$$

1. cont'd.

where $\mu = -\log \mu_{..}$, $\alpha_i = \log \mu_{i.}$ and $\beta_j = \log \mu_{.j}$.

If we now add interaction terms γ_{ij} between category i of variable 1 and category j of variable 2 we get the link function

$$\eta_{ij} = \mu + \alpha_i + \beta_j + \gamma_{ij} .$$

Independence of the variables implies zero interaction terms γ_{ij} which can now be tested.

Polynomial effects in both categories can be modelled by letting

$$\alpha_i = \alpha + \alpha_i + \alpha_i^2 + \ldots + \alpha_i^n$$

and

$$\beta_j = \beta + \beta_j + \beta_j^2 + \ldots + \beta_j^n \quad .$$

This will only make sense if the categories are ordered. The analysis can then proceed as usual.

APPENDIX A

Some important definitions and results

1. If $X \sim N(\mu,\sigma^2)$ then

$$E(X) = \frac{1}{\sqrt{2\pi\sigma}} \int_{-\infty}^{\infty} x \exp\left\{-\tfrac{1}{2}\left(\frac{x-\mu}{\sigma}\right)^2\right\} dx\ .$$

If we let $Z = (x-\mu)\sigma$ then

$$E(X) = \frac{1}{\sqrt{2\pi}}\,\sigma \int_{-\infty}^{\infty} (\sigma Z+\mu) e^{-\frac{Z^2}{2}}\, dZ$$

$$= \frac{1}{\sqrt{2\pi}}\,\sigma \int_{-\infty}^{\infty} e^{-\frac{Z^2}{2}}\, dZ \ + \mu \frac{1}{\sqrt{2\pi}} \int_{-\infty}^{\infty} e^{-\frac{Z^2}{2}}\, dZ\ .$$

The first of the above integrals is zero since the integrand, say (Z), has the property that $f(Z) = -f(-Z)$. The second integral clearly equals μ. Hence

$$E(X) = \mu\ .$$

To evaluate $V(X)$ we need $E(X^2)$. Now

$$E(X^2) = \frac{1}{\sqrt{2\pi}} \int_{-\infty}^{\infty} x^2 \ \exp\left\{-\tfrac{1}{2}\left(\frac{x-\mu}{\sigma}\right)^2\right\}$$

and once again letting $Z = (x-\mu)/\sigma$ we have

$$E(X^2) = \frac{1}{\sqrt{2\pi}} \int_{-\infty}^{\infty} (\sigma Z+\mu)^2 e^{-\frac{Z^2}{2}}\, dZ$$

$$= \frac{1}{\sqrt{2\pi}} \int_{-\infty}^{\infty} \sigma^2 Z^2 e^{-\frac{Z^2}{2}}\, dZ + 2\mu\,\sigma \frac{1}{\sqrt{2\pi}} \int_{-\infty}^{\infty} Z e^{-\frac{Z^2}{2}}\, dZ + \mu^2 \frac{1}{\sqrt{2\pi}} \int_{-\infty}^{\infty} e^{-\frac{Z^2}{2}}\, dZ.$$

As above the second term integrates to zero and the last term equals μ^2. The first term is evaluated by integrating by parts and is equal to σ^2. Thus

$$E(X^2) = \sigma^2 + \mu^2$$

and hence

$$V(X) = E(X^2) - E(X) = \sigma^2\ .$$

2. We have

$$C(Y_1, Y_2) = C\left(\sum_{i=1}^{n} a_i X_i\ ,\ \sum_{j=1}^{m} b_j X_j\right)$$

$$= E\left[\left(\sum_{i=1}^{n} a_i X_i\right)\left(\sum_{j=1}^{m} b_j X_j\right)\right] - E\left[\sum_{i=1}^{n} a_i X_i\right] E\left[\sum_{j=1}^{m} b_j X_j\right]$$

$$= E\left[\sum_{i=1}^{n} \sum_{j=1}^{m} a_i b_j X_i X_j\right] - \left(\sum_{i=1}^{n} a_i\ E[X_i]\right)\left(\sum_{j=1}^{m} b_j E[X_j]\right)$$

$$= \sum_{i=1}^{n} \sum_{j=1}^{m} a_i b_j\ E[X_i X_j] - \sum_{i=1}^{n} \sum_{j=1}^{m} a_i b_j\ E[X_i]\ E[X_j]$$

$$= \sum_{i=1}^{n} \sum_{j=1}^{m} a_i b_j\ C(X_i, X_j)$$

as required.

3. Since a χ^2 distribution with ν degrees of freedom is formed by summing the squares of ν standard normal $N(0,1)$ variates the sum of two χ^2 distributions on ν_1 and ν_2 degrees of freedom is also χ^2 but on $\nu_1 + \nu_2$ degrees of freedom.